UNCONFORMED

An Unbound and Unbridled Path to Unstuck Growth

Bryan Orr

Unconformed © copyright 2023 by Bryan Orr. All rights reserved. No part of this book may be reproduced in any form whatsoever, by photography or xerography or by any other means, by broadcast or transmission, by translation into any kind of language, nor by recording electronically or otherwise, without permission in writing from the author, except by a reviewer, who may quote brief passages in critical articles or reviews.

Blue Collar Mind Publishing
Center Hill, Florida

ISBN: 979-8-9884367-0-6
Library of Congress Control Number: 2023909567
Printed in the United States of America
First Printing: 2023

For my grandfather, Papa:

The most resourceful and curious person I've ever known.

They work with tools and drive a truck,

With a grin on their face, they don't give a [hoot],

The value they bring, the work they do,

No matter the challenge, they always pull through.

Contents

Foreword vii
Introduction xi
Papa and the Salvage Yard 1
Equipping Kids With the Tools for Any Vocation 5
What Makes a Rewarding Career? 11
So ... What Do You Do? 15
Unstuckable 23
Raising Autodidacts 33
Experience Before Lecture 49
Repz Make Gainz 53
Don't Take Me to Lunch 57
Head Cartoons 61
Curiosity and Mastery 65
Feedback vs. Validation 71
Critical Contrarianism 75
Taste and Crappy Work 79
Parting Words 85
Appendix 89
Acknowledgments 93
About the Author 97

Foreword

Bryan Orr is kind of a big deal.

While there is an inside joke in that line, and Bryan likely laughed (after he winced) when he first read it, I also believe it deeply. After you read this book, you will, too. (And you'll get the joke.)

From where I sit, it seems Bryan has turned self-consciousness into self-improvement. His daily work helps others to do the same. Indeed, this book is an example of Bryan raising our collective consciousness to improve society overall, with a specific focus on how we learn and how we perceive our work.

That may sound high-minded or agenda-driven, but it is not. When it comes to how he wishes the world to be, Bryan is not pushing specific answers so much as he is posing incisive questions. And he does so accessibly, humbly, often humorously—and always with profound gratitude.

When you remove the labels and ignore the boxes into which we put our learning and labor, our pedagogy and professions, there are some fundamental truths that this book concisely and compellingly explores.

For instance, if you describe the daily tasks of a skilled, experienced HVAC technician, you will find healthy doses of engineering, artistry, entrepreneurship, and empowerment. And, as Bryan points out, this is but one of many trades where the path to mastery and success is accessible, affordable, and even fun.

In my field of real estate (development, sales, maintenance, and finance), entrepreneurship is everywhere. More often than not, the top professionals in the space did not study their current field in college. They found success by learning from failure—hardhat on and sleeves rolled up. They hustled humbly and took joy in the journey.

In Bryan's work—his teaching, his podcasts, his daily conversations—he helps others find their way to this type of non-traditional path as he reminds us of how traditional such a path once was.

To benefit future generations, Bryan includes advice for raising kids (he is a father of 10!) who will learn to help and teach themselves. As with any great advice for kids, we adults would do well to take it ourselves.

So, regardless of whether you are a teenager, raising teenagers, or old enough to remember a time when college was not the assumed path for all teenagers, I think you will gain insight and inspiration from the pages ahead.

I certainly did.

Enjoy. Spread the word. Hand your tattered copy to another, and ask them to pay it forward as well.

Together, we can regain some scholastic balance and reposition the trades to their rightful place in society.

And if you tune in to the podcast, you'll pick up some handy dad jokes, too.

M. Ryan Gorman
Co-Founder of btcRE LLC
Former CEO of Coldwell Banker, NRT, and Anywhere Advisors
May 2023

Hard work, dedication to one's craft, and the mastery of skills are the foundations upon which societies are built and sustained.

~ Aristotle

Introduction

My wife Leilani and I are the homeschooling parents of ten kids. That's right—ten big, medium, and small bundles of (mostly) joy. Let's be honest: Leilani does the majority of the work. She and I were both home-educated in the 1980s, back when the truant officers would come around and ask why you weren't in school. Attitudes about home education were—how shall I say it? A tad bit negative? It's a much different world now, a much more accepting world. In fact, these days, when I tell people we're homeschooling, they usually shrug and say, "Okay, who isn't?"

My home education served me well. Thanks to my parents and my extended family, I learned essential skills in things that may sound fancy. However, in reality, I was just a kid doing chores and playing. I gained experience in everything from avionics to horticulture, animal husbandry, machine maintenance and repair, household and business management, electrical repair, plumbing, HVACR, and then some.

All of it was a limited, child-like experience of doing and being exposed to skills and how the world works, not a comprehensive course. I learned all that in addition to the three Rs. It may not have been a well-rounded education in the traditional sense, but it worked for me.

I graduated high school when I was just sixteen. Like many newly minted high-school grads, I struggled with deciding what might be next for me. My dad, who is college educated, saw me having trouble figuring out what I wanted to do and gave me the best piece of career advice I've ever received.

"Why don't you learn a trade?" Dad suggested. "Then, no matter what happens, you'll always have that to fall back on. A trade is something nobody can ever take away from you."

"Well, isn't that true of college, too?" I replied. "Nobody can take your degree away from you, either."

Dad went on to explain that a difference exists between knowing a hard skill (sometimes also called *technical skill*: a skill related to a specific job) and knowing about something more ambiguous, which is what many college degrees end up being. He said he had no doubt that I had the ability to do well in college, but at my age, choosing a major and going into student loan debt would be a giant gamble.

I barely knew who I was, let alone what I wanted to do for the rest of my working life. By learning a trade, I would not only come away with valuable, marketable skills, but I would also be giving myself the gift of time—time to figure out my natural inclinations and talents. Time to grow and mature. Time to discover what I find rewarding. Then, if I wanted to, I could go to college and confidently pick a major that suited me. And since I would be earning money while learning and working my trade, I could save up enough to pay for that degree myself, debt-free.

> **"Why don't you learn a trade?" Dad suggested. "Then, no matter what happens, you'll always have that to fall back on."**

I couldn't come up with an argument against Dad's idea. It just made sense. I followed his advice and chose to go to trade school to pursue heating, ventilation, and air conditioning (HVAC). I was drawn to HVAC because it is rich in science and has some challenging and magical problems to solve. The more I learned about it, the more fascinated I became.

Introduction

In the skilled trades, we find the intersection of mind and body, where the power of thought and the precision of hands converge to create the tangible.

~ Matthew B. Crawford,
Shop Class as Soulcraft: An
Inquiry Into the Value of Work

And that's how I transformed from a teen with a fuzzy future into a full-blown HVAC nerd exploring the refrigeration cycle, controls, how heat is absorbed and rejected, how pressure affects temperature, and so on. There was so much to learn! I couldn't get enough.

I worked as an HVAC tech at a large company for several years, then became a trainer of HVAC techs and later a manager. So although I never did make it to college, I'm grateful that I traded the benefits of the trades for the debt and, admittedly, some of the fun of college.

These days, I co-own Kalos Services, a contracting business in central Florida that I started with my dad and uncle. We do general contracting, electrical contracting, HVAC, refrigeration, controls, plumbing, and other construction-related things. Our goal has been to have most of the trades under one roof, making Kalos a one-stop shop for residential and commercial customers.

Kalos currently has more than 200 employees and a training program that mixes classroom education and field experience to give our trainees the opportunity to master their crafts. I also developed a free training website for tradespeople, HVAC School (www.hvacrschool.com), which I call "a place to learn some things you've forgotten along the way as well as remind you of some of the things you forgot to know in the first place." It offers courses, self-learning resources, videos, and a podcast with interesting guests who are experts in the trades—and in life.

Through Kalos, we provide good jobs and upward mobility for hundreds of employees, and it serves a need in our community. Plus, I'm able to provide an enjoyable life for my family. And it all started because my dad gave me permission to explore my options when it came to building a career. He and my other mentors encouraged me to color outside the lines and not blindly follow the culturally prescribed path to "success." What an incredible gift they gave me!

> **I've concluded that the traditional educational model has a lot of room for improvement.**

I want more people to receive this gift. I've trained many folks through Kalos and HVAC School, which has taught me what tends to work and what doesn't. Considering my personal experience doing that sort of training, plus my own home education and the homeschooling Leilani and I have done with our ten children, I've concluded that the traditional educational model has a lot of room for improvement. We need that paradigm to shift in a new direction so that more people can thrive and learn to do work that brings them joy and fulfillment. Not only would that lead to greater numbers of happier people, but it would also lead to stronger communities and a more prosperous world.

This book is a manifesto for transforming the way we think about education so that each person has the opportunity to gain experience and knowledge and build skills that match their unique preferences and talents instead of automatically being herded toward a potentially frustrating career and student loan debt. It is about promoting different ways of approaching education that are quite successful but not as traditionally prestigious.

The idea I'm promoting is not new. It fell out of favor over the past couple of generations because it didn't serve the desires of the large corporations

Introduction

now running the show. The Powers That Be tend to want to create a populace that fulfills their purposes—a populace that works well in factories, a populace taught to question little in exchange for a paycheck. A cookie-cutter populace. The traditional education models are good at pumping out folks who fit that description. And no, I'm not a conspiracy theorist. I'm just someone who has read and thought a lot about this. Most importantly, my family and I have lived the inverse.

To prove that I'm not a tin-foil-hat-wearing conspiracist, I'll tell you the story of how our current system came to exist. Back in the late 1800s and early 1900s, as the Industrial Revolution rolled across America, an inventor and mechanical engineer in Philadelphia named Frederick W. Taylor was busy devising ways to make manufacturing more efficient. After completing an apprenticeship as a patternmaker, he took a job as a shop clerk and machinist in a steel company, gradually working his way up the ranks until he became chief engineer. As he carried out each of the many jobs he held, he became fascinated with the manufacturing process and how to make it more efficient and effective.

Over time, he developed a system of industrial management that closely monitored each worker to reduce wasted time and motion. It was pretty darn unpopular with the line workers (seriously, who among us enjoys being scrutinized by their bosses all day, every day?). Still, the positive effect on the bottom line was undeniable.

Suddenly, Taylor's management system, dubbed "Taylorism," was all the rage in the industrial world. Ultimately, Taylor became a consulting engineer to various U.S. manufacturers, including giant Bethlehem Steel. American factory workers learned to march in lockstep like tin soldiers if they wanted to keep their jobs.

> *It is only through enforced standardization of methods, enforced adoption of the best implements and working*

conditions, and enforced cooperation that this faster work can be assured. And the duty of enforcing the adoption of standards and enforcing this cooperation rests with management alone.

~Frederick W. Taylor,
The Principles of Scientific Management

During the same period that Frederick Taylor was establishing efficiency standards for the workforce, John Dewey, a philosopher and educational reformer, was advocating for a new approach to education that came to be known as "progressive education." This philosophy was not necessarily intended to "standardize" children but did focus on standardizing the educational model. Dewey's philosophy emphasized the importance of education serving society's needs, which were largely industrial.

Learning how to learn is more important than what you learn.

While it is a stretch to claim that Dewey's educational approach was specifically designed to prepare students for work in industrial factories, it did emphasize skills that were crucial to an industrialized society at the time.

Today, as we've transitioned from an industrial economy to a more knowledge-based one, it is reasonable to suggest that our educational approaches should similarly grow and change. While manufacturing and industry remain important sectors, we face an increasing demand for critical thinking, creativity, and digital literacy skills.

Therefore, the issue is not so much about "winding back" Dewey's system but rather about continuing to adapt and change our educational practices to meet the current needs of our society. We should remember: **The objective of education is not to fit students into predefined molds but to equip them with the knowledge and skills they need to navigate an ever-**

Introduction

changing world. In this context, learning how to learn is more important than what you learn.

So am I arguing that college is a waste of time and money and that no one should ever take that route? Absolutely not! Countless university-educated people are successful. But for many, it wasn't their degree that led to their success. The degree may have been just one layer they built upon using the time-tested methods, tips, tricks, and inspiration I will describe in this book. My message is that for people who are not yet sure what they want to do, those who love working with their hands, those for whom higher education might not be a good fit, or those who have the degree(s) but who are still wondering why "success" has eluded them, there is another way forward.

You may be a parent, grandparent, guidance counselor, business leader, or influencer of young people. If so, you can give the kids in your care the gift my family gave me by opening their eyes to all the different paths for finding their personal True North when it comes to making a living. Correction: Let's change that to "when it comes to making a *life*."

You can even give yourself this gift. If you are older and feeling unfulfilled in your education or career, this book also has a message for you. I will give you some interesting (and maybe slightly unconventional) ideas in the pages ahead. I'm going to explore:

- What really makes for a rewarding career
- The four tools kids need to be able to succeed in *any* vocation, and how you can help equip them
- Why it's crucial to "shotgun before you laser"
- What Ben Franklin, Leonardo da Vinci, Maya Angelou, and your kid have in common

- How the modern apprenticeship model is setting up more people for success

- The value of *just-in-time learning*

- Why the plumber may be less "stuck" in their career than the attorney (Hint: It has nothing to do with the plumber's easy access to plungers)

- Feedback versus validation, and why it's important to teach your kids—and maybe even yourself—the difference

- Why I don't want you to take me to lunch

In addition to all that, you'll hear from my friends Kimberly Llewellyn, Senior Product Manager for Mitsubishi Electric Trane, and Ryan Gorman, former CEO of Coldwell Banker real estate. They have both been on my podcast and discussed this topic with me. Each brings the perspective of an accomplished, college-educated professional who sees the dangers of a single educational approach and the importance of skilled workers of all types.

> "I think it's really important for us to challenge the narrative that college is the only path to success in American society."

Now, let me reiterate: The point of this book (and my argument) is *not* to undercut the value of college education or white-collar careers. I am not trying to persuade people who want to go to college to pick up tools instead. I merely concur with Ryan Gorman's belief about college as it pertains to career preparation, which he shared with me during one of my podcasts.

"I don't think there should never be college," Ryan said, "but I do think it's a massively overprescribed medication that people just take without really thinking too deeply about it."

Introduction

Kimberly said it this way when we discussed the common ideas about going to college. "I think it's really important for us to challenge the narrative that college is the only path to success in American society. We need to acknowledge and value the critical skill sets and knowledge that come from field-based work and make sure that those jobs are well-compensated and respected."

Like Kimberly and Ryan, I want everyone—kids, young people, and mature adults alike—to feel hopeful that viable and rewarding careers are waiting for them even if they don't go to college. I'll focus a lot on the kids here, but almost everything I have to say applies to people of all ages. So, let's explore how anyone can prepare for a satisfying, lucrative career, no matter what educational or training path they end up choosing.

1 Papa and the Salvage Yard

I've got this mental image of my grandfather engraved in my mind's eye. He's in his office at his aircraft hangar, leaning back in his chair with his hands behind his head, laughing, joking, and swapping stories with one of his customers. The customers have universally loved him, and the feeling has always been mutual. He was (and is) a great businessman but not in the conventional sense. He's not a business process builder or a devisor of corporate systems. Instead, he's an opportunistic thinker—a problem solver who can dive full force into any opportunity that comes along and do it with great vigor and joy. How he got there is a pretty cool story.

My grandfather, Don Huntington—whom I call Papa—was born in Bedford, Ohio, in 1943 during World War II in the aftermath of the Great Depression. He is no stranger to hard work. He started working in a small coal mine at the ripe old age of six after being forced into the job by his father. I can't imagine what life must have been like for him. But as Papa tells it, it was easier to be a little boy working in a coal mine than to be a little boy at home with his abusive dad.

Papa decided at a young age that he didn't want to be anything like his father. He married my grandmother when they were both very young and set about building a good life for his new family. Since then, he's done practically every kind of job you can imagine. He worked as an electrician, a machinist, a well driller, and in water treatment. He was a scuba-diving plumber at Disney World, for Pete's sake—who knew that was even a thing? By the time he was forty, he had done around forty different jobs, all with only an eighth-grade education and a lot of difficulty reading because of severe dyslexia.

My grandfather has always had a fascination with aviation. He learned to fly while still in Ohio and brought that love with him when he moved to Florida. The year I was born, he decided to build his own airplane from a kit—a Long-EZ aircraft designed by Burt Rutan, the designer who engineered the first aircraft to circumnavigate the globe non-stop.

Papa quickly realized that he would need a lot of parts to build that plane. Rather than buying them new, though, he decided he would just buy some wrecked planes, pull what he needed off them, and sell whatever parts remained. That's how his business, Quality Aircraft Salvage, started.

I grew up with a photo of the Voyager (the plane flew non-stop around the world) on the wall of my room at home while also riding around the country with Papa scouting for airplanes, tearing them apart, and bringing them back to his salvage yard in Groveland, Florida, where he sold the parts he didn't need.

I was around twelve when he finally finished building his plane. It was one of his many interests, and through it, he developed a set of exceptional skills.

By the time his airplane construction project was complete, he had built a thriving salvage business. Most of Papa's sales happened over the phone or by fax, but people would sometimes fly in from all around the country and bargain with him over parts. He was the consummate haggler. As I watched him work, I learned that business is about relationships. Years later, one of my business coaches, Rick Corbin, said it best:

Business is, in its truest form, an excuse to be in a relationship with one another.

My grandfather really knew how to build relationships.

To keep me busy at the salvage yard, Papa would have me do little tasks like sorting bolts, sealing parts in plastic bags, and shredding the paper he used as packing material for shipping his goods. I also worked with him from a young age at his booth at the annual Sun and Fun Fly-In Air Show in nearby Lakeland, Florida, where he would always give me something to sell on my own. One year, it was these wooden walnuts that, when you opened them, contained a little bug. You'd open the walnut, and the bug's legs would suddenly start wiggling and twitching. Everybody would scream and throw them down—then step up with handfuls of cash to buy the nuts as gag gifts for their family and friends.

> **My grandfather gave me a special opportunity to experience things at a young age that most kids don't get to do.**

I got the chance to meet many interesting people at the air shows. Whenever someone from another country stopped by our booth, Papa would ask them for a couple of small bills or coins in their native currency, and he'd give them to me. Back at home, I would look up where the money came from and learn about those places. Over time, I built up a collection of currencies from all around the world. It was a ton of fun.

Even though he had very little formal education, Papa was an early adopter of technology. He bought me my first computer, an IBM 286, and allowed me to play educational games like Reader Rabbit and Math Blaster on them. Whenever a new computer model came out, he bought it for me.

My grandfather gave me a special opportunity to experience things at a young age that most kids don't get to do. First, because I was homeschooled, I got to spend a lot of time with him. Second, because my grandfather was a traditional old-school self-learner (what I call an autodidact—more on that later!), he didn't set out to seek education just for education's sake. He pursued his interests, learning whatever he needed to learn along the way, and in the process, he became well-educated in many different things. He became somebody people relied on to help them solve problems.

Papa always encouraged me to work hard, try new things, and meet new people. He saw every experience and interaction as an opportunity for learning. I didn't realize it at the time, but by teaching me the art of the deal and the value of relationships, curiosity, and hard work, my grandfather was preparing me for my future. He was giving me the basic tools I would need to have a happy, fulfilling life at work, at home, and in my community—which brings me to the next chapter.

2 Equipping Kids With the Tools for Any Vocation

As the homeschooling dad of ten kids, I know that some of the most effective education starts at the kitchen table with the child who's rubbing their eyes and mumbling, "I don't want to learn this." It then moves into the dirt, the grease, and the real-life stuff we do with our kids, much like Papa did with me at the salvage yard and air show booths. These are the kinds of "labs" where kids can experiment and learn the things they need to know to be productive and fulfilled—labs where they are free to make mistakes and practice their reps.

> **We want our children to acknowledge that they can always grow.**

I know from experience that it can feel overwhelming trying to make sure you cover all the bases with your kids so that they will thrive—not just function—in adulthood. That's why I devised a simple, big-picture place to start. It may sound a little "woo-woo" to you at first, but please stick with me. We have to ground ourselves in this understanding before we can answer more detailed questions about what to give our children to prepare them for any vocation.

What I want most for my children—heck, for *every* person—are these four things:

Character
Growth
Joy
Purpose

The sky is the limit for people with these four qualities. Let's take them one by one.

We all know what it looks like when someone has **character**. They do the right thing. They have integrity. They're compassionate and fair. They're dependable and responsible. They're just an all-around good citizen. But how do we instill character in our children? I've thought about this a lot as I've been working and training people, and eventually, it came to me.

You've got to have high standards.

C. S. Lewis once wrote, "God is easy to please, but impossible to satisfy." As parents, striking a balance between being pleased and satisfied is always a challenge. We don't want to be impossible to satisfy in the sense that we expect our kids to knock themselves out all the time trying to live up to our impossible critique or to experience anxiety about our expectations. But we want our children to acknowledge that they can always grow. We can want more for our children than what they have and where they are right now.

That does not mean, however, that we should be difficult to please—or that their goals should even be to please us. It means we hold them to high standards for effort and engagement, for getting in there and doing the right thing. But we can set lower expectations for performance because, after all, they are *kids*. We don't want to be like the dad who looks at his five-year-old's drawing and says, "Really? This is supposed to be a giraffe? Looks like a goat to me. The neck is not nearly long enough. Try harder!"

That is definitely *not* what Jesus would do!

Be willing to praise effort and then give feedback on what the next journey of growth looks like. Celebrate the now and point to the next.

As parents, we can't force-feed our kids' lifelong goals. That's not how it's going to happen. In fact, if we try to force-feed anything to our children, they will end up resenting it. Whether it's about sports, grades, a career, college, or anything else, if you try to impose something on your kids, it becomes an expectation. Expectations lead to disappointment, burnout, frustration, and resentment. That's all they do. So when it comes to character building, don't have expectations—have standards.

In our family, we treat people with respect. We always do our best. We work hard. We finish what we start. We leave things better than we found them. These are standards. You could also call them norms. Standards are impersonal; they're aimed at "us" as a collective. In contrast, expectations are personal; they're aimed at *you*. Standards are something we all agree to sign on to—a common goal we are working towards. Expectations, on the other hand, create interpersonal pressure.

See the difference? If you set a standard and a kid doesn't meet it, you can do something about it. But if you have an expectation and the kid "fails" to satisfy it, there is nothing you can do but be disappointed.

The next tool children need is a **growth mindset**, which is a mindset of lifelong learning. Lifelong learning is a phrase I use a lot, mostly with adults, because we tend to lose that mentality with age. You get your certificate, you follow your course, you get your degree, and now you've made it, right?

Nope. We all know that's not how it works. We're always going to have to learn new stuff. The world keeps speeding up, and the things we learned ten years ago often become irrelevant. Just think about how much technology has changed since, um, I don't know—yesterday? Approaching new learning opportunities with fear or a defeatist attitude gets a person nowhere fast. So we have to encourage our kids to adopt a mindset of lifelong learning and growth, and that starts with embracing it ourselves.

> **As parents, we have the opportunity to feed them opportunities for growth so that they can build a broad portfolio of skills.**

Rather than thinking of education as linear, let's think of it as helping our kids build a portfolio of skills. The foundation of creating a wide range of useful skills is having a habit of applying them. As parents, we can help our kids develop a habit of learning. If a child gets into the habit of playing four hours of video games every day, then that's what they will be good at. That's what they're going to give themselves to.

We can help them see the power of habit by modeling good practices of our own. It all comes down to what you feed them. As parents, we have the opportunity to feed them opportunities for growth so that they can build a broad portfolio of skills that will serve them well now and in the future, no matter what vocation they choose.

Next, we want to equip our kids with a sense of **joy**—joy in work and joy in learning. Whether it's serving others, whether it's the job we do every day, whether it's serving our children by educating them, if we aren't expressing joy in what we do, then who wants to be us?

Think back to when you were a kid. You could tell when your parents were not experiencing joy. How did that make you feel? Even if you were doing something you loved, if your parents weren't happy, then it didn't feel the same. On the other hand, when you knew that they felt joy in what they were doing with you (or doing for themselves), it made all the difference.

I was presenting and exhibiting at a conference a few years ago, and one of our sons, who was five at the time, was helping me in our booth. He and I were having a blast interacting with the people who stopped by. And then, with this huge grin on his face, he started telling people that I "owned this conference hall" we were standing in.

"Yeah, my dad owns this place!" he declared.

I had to laugh. While I clearly never said I owned the place, maybe I was acting like I did (gulp). It was fun to see him feeding off my excitement over what we were doing. I cherish those kinds of experiences together.

And finally, people need a **purpose**. We need to feel that what we are doing matters and has meaning—this is especially true for the younger generations. We'll discuss this again in the next chapter, but for now, let's just say that purpose is a worthwhile goal. But for many, purpose is an abstract concept. It is elusive. Some people have trouble figuring out what their Big-Picture Purpose is.

I think that's because we often encourage or expect young people to find it too early. When you're a kid, the only things you can see are the bright shiny objects—like becoming an astronaut, a YouTuber, a pro athlete, or a billionaire like Mark Cuban or Oprah Winfrey. But what they don't understand is that Cuban and Winfrey are billionaires because they actually know things and do things and are excited about them. They learned and did a lot of small stuff in order to build up to the big accomplishments.

So rather than promoting the idea of discovering their macro purpose, perhaps we ought to guide our children toward solving smaller problems that help them develop character, growth, and joy. Those small sandboxes they play in—building a city out of blocks, planting a garden, fixing a lawnmower, singing a song, changing a tire, getting that first car up and running— are the micro-purposes that lead to macro-purpose and lifelong satisfaction. Approaching it the other way around is putting the cart before the horse. We want that cart, of course, but first, we must practice the modalities by which we're going to discover it. That requires character, a mindset of growth, and joy.

Our role as parents is to create opportunities and structures for our children to equip themselves with character, growth, joy, and purpose. Every vocation, avocation, and profession is available to the joyful person with character, a purpose, and a commitment to lifelong growth. If you've ever been responsible for hiring or training people, you know that's true. If you're hiring and you come across a candidate who is joyful, has great character, a purpose, and a commitment to lifelong learning—but doesn't have the right piece of paper—are you going to pass them by so you can hire the unpleasant person with the right piece of paper who seems likely to gossip and complain? Of course not. I'm not saying that certificates and degrees and higher education aren't valuable, but they're icing on the cake.

> **Perhaps we ought to guide our children toward solving smaller problems that help them develop character, growth, and joy.**

First comes character, growth, joy, and purpose.

In today's world, these four tools are like superpowers. They are so rare. Let's do everything we can to change that.

3 What Makes a Rewarding Career?

What makes for a rewarding career? I love this question. If you ask a Millennial or Gen Z'er what makes a career rewarding, *purpose* is one of the most common answers. They want *meaning*.

Then you ask them, "So, what job do you want to do?"

"I want to be an engineer," they reply.

"You mean like the guy or gal with the stripy hat who drives the trains?"

They chuckle and roll their eyes, having already heard the same line from every dad joker they've met.

"No, not that kind of engineer," they say.

"Okay then, what kind of an engineer do you want to be?"

"I'm not sure…"

"Well, do you enjoy math? Engineers do a lot of math."

"No, I don't like math," they say. "I like building things."

"So, do you want to start by being an engineer, or do you want to start by building things?"

"Building things, I think."

"Cool! You can start by building things, which is something you already know you like doing. After that, if you still want to become an engineer, you can."

"But I already know I want to be an engineer."

"Okay, but why? What makes you so sure?"

The odds are good that if you dig deep enough in this line of questioning, you'll find out they want to be an engineer because they were told they should be an engineer. Is that a good enough reason for them to head to engineering school and rack up a mountain of student loan debt to do a job they might not even like?

Look, I'm not saying the kid should *not* be an engineer. I want to be really clear about this. I'm not knocking college. But I am knocking the system because the system needs an overhaul. It just does. Everybody knows it, even the people inside the system. So we should improve the system, we should improve college, and we should improve what higher education looks like.

> **If you dig deep enough in this line of questioning, you'll find out they want to be an engineer because they were told they should be an engineer.**

The good news is that more people are open to that right now, and we have the Coronavirus pandemic to thank for it. Parents were paying the same amount of tuition to have their kids do Zoom classes during the lockdowns as they were to have them on campus before the pandemic, and they started to realize, *Hey, wait a second. This is kind of a scam, isn't it?*

What Makes a Rewarding Career?

The entire system is built to give out pieces of paper to say, "You are good enough. You are smart enough." But everybody knows that **skills** are what matter. They are the only things that matter in the marketplace.

For a career to be rewarding, young people need the chance to develop and use their skills to solve interesting and meaningful problems. They also need a diversity of challenges, which means they are not stuck solving the same problem over and over again. They want to have an impact.

That desire to have an impact is a powerful motivation, especially for kids who are more relational and social. They want to **know** that they're changing the world for good rather than **to be seen** *seeming* to change the world for good. There's a key distinction there.

My friend Mike and I talk about this all the time. He and I went on a mission trip to Haiti together, and both our families are involved in missions. We have to walk a fine line between doing good because we love serving and doing good so that we can be seen looking like we're doing good. It comes down to doing the work in service to others versus doing the work in service to our ego.

> **Everybody knows that skills are what matter.**

That is a conversation we should be having with our children on a regular basis—not a conversation that discourages them from doing good, but a dialogue that encourages them to do good in a way that is not about being seen as much as it is about serving.

Now, what does this have to do with a rewarding career for your child? It's simple: A career will be more rewarding for them when it gives them the opportunity to serve in a way that's meaningful for them and not just the opportunity to have a prestigious title that makes other people sit up and take notice.

Many of the jobs with super prestigious titles—jobs that seem like they would be a lot of fun—often lack human connection. We are wired to connect—some of us more so than others. For children who thrive on building and maintaining relationships, this is critical. You wouldn't want to put them into a position where they're not getting the meaningful connections they crave.

It all boils down to helping your child understand the intersection between their natural inclinations and interests and the reality of any career they're considering. It may even involve opening their eyes to previously unexplored options that might be a perfect match.

For example, if you have a task-oriented child with a problem-solving mind, reinforce the importance of finding a vocation that presents interesting and meaningful problems for them to solve. If your child is a super-social team player, help them learn more about career options that put those strengths to good use. That will be so much more freeing than picking something strictly on the basis of prestige—or what Grandpa thinks.

4 So ... What Do You Do?

The lobby of the event center is crowded and hot. My jacket is too stiff around the shoulders, and my white dress shirt collar is so tight that my face looks like a red zit ready to pop.

Whose idea of fashion was a suit and tie? I wonder. Grumbling under my breath, I ask myself, *Why the heck am I even here?*

My wife pauses for a second to shoot me a pitying glance as she converses easily with friends and acquaintances from the community.

It's not that I don't like people. I do. It's just that I struggle with small talk. And in a place like this, small talk is the currency of social ease. I have a hard time transitioning from small talk to substantial conversation without making it awkward, especially when I'm in a group composed of mostly traditionally educated, white-collar professionals. I imagine them asking me, "What do you do?" and when I tell them, I figure they will immediately conclude that they are superior to me. *What could they possibly gain from*

> **We parents always want to say we're proud of our kids, but it's amazing how much more proud people seem when their kids go to college.**

having a conversation with me—a homeschooled, blue-collar Average Joe?

I feel much more comfortable in the company of tradespeople with whom I have an authentic connection based on common experience and understanding. I don't like the transactional nature of modern Western business "networking," where people are just looking for the value they can extract rather than how they can serve or express genuine interest in what another person does. All that networking feels like it's about accumulating superficial connections rather than forming meaningful relationships.

Thankfully, I've (mostly) overcome my inferiority complex, but it's important for me to tell you about it. My experience might help you if one or more of your kids decides to take something other than the traditional educational path.

We parents always want to say we're proud of our kids, but it's amazing how much **more** proud people seem when their kids go to college. When their kid is pursuing a medical degree, people seem a lot more willing to share what their child is doing with their life than, say, when their child is an apprentice plumber.

I get it. I suffer from the same thing, which is ironic because I preach this. I will admit that if one of my kids went to Harvard Business School, I'd probably be far more prone to brag about that than my 21-year-old son, a market refrigeration tech making great money and owning his own home. It's crazy that even *I* feel that social pressure! It's all about the cocktail hour with our friends and how we allow their values and worldviews to affect us.

Not long ago, I gave a talk at HARDI, one of the major events tailored for the bigwigs of the HVACR industry. I was invited to participate in a panel discussion as the token tradesperson. At one point, the topic turned to professionalism in the industry, and someone asked why there weren't more "quality people" going into the trades. Boy, did I jump on *that* question!

"Before I answer you, I have a question for everyone in this room," I said, addressing the audience of about 200 people. "By a show of hands, how many of you actively encourage your children to go into the trades rather than pursuing a college education?"

Three people raised a hand.

Point made.

As a society, we often think tradespeople, craftspeople, and artisans are second-class citizens, and we treat them that way. We would never think of calling our lawyer and saying, "Hey, can I pick your brain real quick?" without expecting to receive a bill for their time. But we have no problem calling our buddy who's an AC technician and asking him if we can pick his brain, keeping him on the phone for an hour, and then complaining when he charges $300 to replace a part we "could buy on Amazon for thirty dollars" yet have no idea how to install. We don't tell the doctor that we could have done that outpatient surgery ourselves for ten dollars. Obviously, we couldn't have—but what a ridiculous thing to say.

> **We don't tell the doctor that we could have done that outpatient surgery ourselves for ten dollars.**

Sadly, it has become socially acceptable to make people feel bad for earning a comfortable living doing our landscaping, putting on our roofs, or installing our insulation. We feel it's our right not only to disparage those folks but to browbeat them when they don't charge prices we like. And then we wonder why they don't act like professionals.

This mindset reveals a fundamental issue with how we look at other people and goes beyond even where they are right now. Kimberly Llewellyn explains it well:

> *If we don't value the person pushing the broom on a job site or in a school, what we are saying is, "That job doesn't matter. It's not important."*

We know that's not true. Seemingly menial tasks, like broom pushing, are essential to keeping a job site clean and safe. Whether that person will always push a broom or is actively acquiring skills and experience that will lead to different roles and responsibilities, that job is still essential, and the broom pusher should, accordingly, be treated with respect.

Our society tends to have a lack of respect for tradespeople and manual labor, and that's why many of us would be embarrassed (or, at the very least, reluctant to talk about it) if our kid ended up in the trades or other critically important jobs.

Taking the opinions of our peers to heart and competing with them over whose kids are succeeding or failing is not only wrong but dangerous.

Taking the opinions of our peers to heart and competing with them over whose kids are succeeding or failing is not only wrong but dangerous. It's dangerous because it hurts our children. It holds them back. It negatively affects our relationship with them, and it's bad for society.

So what if your neighbor's kid is getting a law degree from Harvard while your kid is a musician or plumber? Aren't those equally fine options? We know, deep down, that the answer is yes. Yet we still have to fight that competitive drive, that subjective definition of success that influences our thinking. We don't want to be failures; we don't want to be losers.

But here's a news flash: neither do our teenagers. It's easy to make them feel like a disappointment to us when we have expectations for what "success" should mean for them. Again, we return to the difference between expectations and standards: Expectations are aimed at *them* and can only lead to disappointment, while standards are impersonal and aimed at *us*.

Good teachers always have high standards, which means that they view their students not as their behaviors but as the possibilities they represent. Everybody represents a much greater possibility than their current behavior might indicate—all of us, even me. My wife often puts this theory into practice with me—when I'm acting like a total jerk, she treats me kindly in the moment and doesn't define me by that. Her way of responding makes me **not** want to be a jerk. When it comes to our kids, if we always make it clear to them that they're not meeting our (or, more likely, our peers') expectations for success—even if we're using acceptably positive language—we're not recognizing the possibilities they represent.

The media present another negative force shaping our views about what we want for our kids and what is best for them. The media tell us all kinds of lies about what a successful young person looks like. If you ask parents what they want for their kids, the most common answer is, "We want them to be happy."

But what does that mean? One definition of happiness is the hedonistic pursuit of pleasure and avoidance of discomfort. If that's the kind of happiness you want for your kids, I have one question: *How's that working out for you?* Countless teenagers have pursued that sort of happiness with their very confused teenage minds, leading to a lot of destruction. Heck, I'm an adult man, and if I were to pursue my own hedonistic happiness first and foremost in the simplest short-term sense, it would undoubtedly lead to destruction.

However, if your definition of happiness is pursuing value, utility, purpose, and contentment, then, by all means, encourage your kids to go for it. Just don't believe the media or let what you see and hear influence your ideas about what is best for your kids.

And then there are grandparents. Thank goodness for them. Grandparents have become a lot more accepting, but issues still arise when it comes to what they think is appropriate for their grandkids.

When I was first homeschooled, one side of the family was cool with it. The other side of the family? Not so much. You may have grandparents who are okay with homeschooling, but in the end, it still boils down to prestige. *What is Bobby doing with his life? Where is he headed?* Translation: *Is our grandson going to make us proud by going to college and pursuing something in the handful of high-status careers—doctor, lawyer, politician, scientist, banker, movie star—that we find acceptable? Or is he going to disappoint us by choosing something else?*

What's interesting is that the traditional careers we think of as prestigious come with some of the greatest baggage. Nearly every day brings news of yet another high-profile person overdosing, getting arrested, or otherwise melting down. Why do you think that is? Many folks get into those types of jobs because they pay well or seem like a big deal, but often, all the glitz and glamour can't hide the fact that this journey they took was not necessarily how that particular person truly wanted to spend their life. They end up feeling like they need to fill the resulting void in their soul with something, and often that "something" is drugs, alcohol, greed, or self-absorption.

> **If your definition of happiness is pursuing value, utility, purpose, and contentment, then, by all means, encourage your kids to go for it.**

A few of them do figure out a healthier way. Take actor Nick Offerman, for instance. His portrayal of Ron Swanson in NBC's *Parks and Recreation* sitcom is what made him famous, but woodworking is what makes him happy. As Offerman puts it: "I'm enjoying the opportunity that *Parks and Recreation* affords me to exploit my own soapbox agenda, which is to try to encourage people to make things with their hands."

It's funny. Once upon a time, the people who made a living working with their hands—artisans, tradespeople, craftspeople—were respected and often even revered. The town blacksmith comes to mind, as does the carpenter, the miller, the printer, the wagon maker, and the stone mason. The village couldn't function without those folks.

The same is true today. Our "village" won't last much longer without skilled tradespeople to build and maintain it. The mindset that only those who can't hack it in college should take up a skilled trade not only hurts the individual but also our society.

Kimberly Llewellyn sees the same things in her work. "What is fundamentally important to society?" she asks, then answers: "The ability to fix problems and create things that are necessary to survival, and these are the same skills that often get demeaned."

On the bright side, I do see some positive movement toward changing the perception of the trades as "low-class." People are beginning to respect blue-collar work more because many people now associate the trades with creativity and DIY culture. Etsy is a great example. People can make money creating jewelry, furniture, or floral arrangements and selling them in their online shops. Those are examples of skilled work, and buyers will admire and pay for the work that goes into those products.

We can also thank social media for showcasing the artistry of blue-collar work. Just look at the many viral building and repair videos on Facebook, TikTok, and other social media outlets, not to mention the satisfying horseshoeing, sheep shearing, and bricklaying compilations. The popularity of shows like *This Old House, The Woodwright's Shop, Dirty Jobs, Craft in America,* and any of the primetime home renovation shows on HGTV are evidence that more people than ever are admiring the work of skilled tradespeople.

I look forward to the day when a young tradesperson can answer the question, "So, what do you do?" with their head held high and get enthusiastic thanks for their efforts. If more parents and grandparents would encourage (and, at the very least, accept) these career options for their offspring, we as a society would get there a lot quicker.

5 Unstuckable

I have a friend whose husband is an artist, a classically trained oil painter who graduated from one of the best art schools in Latin America. His paintings are spectacular. You can tell that this guy really knows what he's doing, but his paintings are more than just pretty pictures. They are sublime—so amazing that when you stand in front of them, you can feel his presence even when he's not in the room. I asked him how he learned to do this.

"In art school, our professors taught us the proper technique, like how to draw, how to hold the brush, how to mix the paint on the palette," he explained. "I practiced these techniques for years until I gained muscle memory and confidence. Eventually, I realized that I had the technical ability to create whatever I wanted on the canvas. I didn't even have to think about the process anymore. It was then that I moved beyond the method and became an artist. *I became free.*"

Ah, freedom! It's something we want for ourselves (and, most especially, for our kids). Freedom is one of the reasons we encourage (and sometimes insist that) our children get an education to enable them to pursue prestigious careers that pay well, like medicine, the law, finance, or engineering. We're afraid that if they don't go to college, they'll be stuck in a dead-end job like plumbing or welding for the rest of their lives—that they'll be what many people perceive as the *opposite* of free.

But what if, instead of automatically steering kids toward college, we empowered them to build applicable knowledge and skills in something that interested them: something they could continue to be curious about? I would wish for them to be able, like my artist friend, to get beyond the strictly physical manifestation of their work, comprehend the underpinnings of it, and become world-class experts in what they do—and also to be well compensated for their efforts. No expensive university degree would be required.

> **It was then that I moved beyond the method and became an artist. *I became free*.**

Most of us seem to understand that, in the arts, there is no piece of paper, no certificate that tells you or anyone else how talented you are—or that you're "approved" to do what you do. You don't need a committee to review your work to say that you're "good enough." The art itself does that. The quality of your work is proof of the talent and skill you developed through practice and laboring through the hard moments, sustained by the passion and joy of doing work that suits you.

Kimberly introduced me to a quote from the Roman architect and engineer Vitruvius, a man whose many ancient buildings still stand:

> *They read in the books written by the old masters on architecture, that in planning public and private buildings, regard is to be had to what is appropriate to the dignity and purpose of each; but what is meant by "appropriate" they cannot understand, because they do not know what is "reality" in things, or how it is to be found. Hence, while they devote their energy to the branches of learning, they fail to acquire "reality," which is the chief thing of all. As a result, in their designs for buildings of every kind, they draw colonnades, construct facades, and express their*

> *principles in the symmetry of their work, but there is no real result.*

So in building something truly lasting, you're not "chasing the shadow rather than the substance," as Vitruvius put it, with the shadow being the theoretical understanding that garners the approval of others. You're doing it because you're committed to the substance and to developing your skills in reality.

That's freedom. That doesn't sound like being "stuck" to me.

It's a mistake to think that the plumber or welder is stuck. I would say that the lawyer—the person who spends six to eight years and hundreds of thousands of dollars earning a Juris Doctor degree only to realize a few years later that they don't like the job—is more stuck than the plumber or welder. I've spoken to many engineers, doctors, lawyers, and others with high-level degrees who, although they're proud of their degree and the work they've done, often say they feel trapped in a career they never really wanted.

On the flip side of the coin are the thousands of tradespeople and artisans I've met who are happy to be doing rewarding work that suits them. Many of these people knew from the get-go that they wanted a career working with their hands. They bypassed higher education and started as soon as they were old enough. Others went to college, didn't like it (or couldn't figure out what to study), and then decided to go in a different direction.

My stance is that you should consider shotgunning before you laser. It's good for young people to go wide before they go narrow, as that gives them enough perspective and real-world knowledge to understand their true inclinations and talents. The problem is that our traditional educational model doesn't afford most people that opportunity. You come out of high school barely knowing who you are, and you're shoved directly into the expensive world of higher education. That's a major—and potentially costly—gamble.

In the past, young adults used to travel abroad to gain knowledge and experience before earning a degree. Some still do today, but that option is often only available to those in certain economic classes. I advocate a different version of traveling abroad. How about "traveling near": trying out different jobs and experiencing diverse things during young adulthood?

After our 18-year-old son graduated high school and worked for us for a little bit, he went out to Wyoming and Colorado and did a wide range of jobs for a while. He learned the fundamental skills of taking care of himself while working hard and earning his own money. Who's to say he won't still become a doctor or a lawyer someday? Maybe he will. If he does, I'm certain he'll be a more well-rounded doctor or lawyer with a diverse set of skills he learned as a young man.

If a young person wants to pursue the arts or anything else that interests them, they should absolutely do that rather than feel like a failure because they don't have it all figured out at the tender age of 18. We should give them that option whenever we can. Why is earning the most you possibly can as quickly as you possibly can—without consideration for your interests, your passions, or going into debt—the accepted value system in our society? I'd like to flip that script so that more young people can experience a lot more learning, freedom, and joy.

> *The labor of the hands ennobles the soul, connecting us to the roots of our humanity and the essence of our existence.*
>
> ~ Leonardo da Vinci

But let's say you have a super-intelligent child (and I know you do!), so you feel as though you *must* suggest or recommend or demand that they go to college to become an engineer or an architect or a lawyer—because they're super intelligent and *they can*. I would argue that every job benefits from intelligent people, and the opportunities for them will be great, no matter what they choose as a career.

An intelligent and curious farmer, machinist, HVAC installer, builder, or roofer is not going to be stuck doing physical labor for the rest of their life unless they choose to. They are going to be **completely unstuck**, able to go anywhere in the world and apply themselves in a variety of ways. Should they want or need to leave their home country for whatever reason, they can take the skills they already have in their tool bag and bring them to their new location.

That said, it's also worth mentioning that there are some folks who are "stuck" in the trades—but they're stuck because they identify themselves as and choose to remain as only one thing. They may say, "I'm only going to be able to do this work (mechanic, AC tech, plumber, etc.) for so long before the job ruins me and my body breaks down." That's *a common mindset of stuckness* that some tradespeople have.

Part of the reason for that mindset is society's lack of respect for the trades and tradespeople. Thankfully, that's changing for the better. Another reason they feel stuck is that they haven't yet figured out that if they are willing to grow and learn and confidently step into the next opportunity, the sky's the limit.

Tradespeople with applicable skills, experience, and a determination to learn can make lateral moves to other trades or other roles in the same trade that might better fit their lifestyle (and no, these other roles aren't only in management). Having a solid foundation of mechanical skills opens many doors for better-paying jobs or ones with more work-life balance.

As you progress in a trades career with an open mind and a willingness to learn, you will find out that your trade goes way beyond just turning a wrench. If you really like turning a wrench, then maybe you can become a trainer or an educator and teach other people to turn a wrench. If you *really love* turning the wrench, maybe you can become a highly valued specialist in a job that allows you to go super deep in a particular discipline and become a AAA world-class expert.

Maybe you can create a YouTube channel and teach others. Maybe you are good with people, so you can develop skills in sales and use the aptitude you've developed in the field to become an expert at selling it. Maybe you could build upon your people skills and trade skills and develop management skills so that you can lead a team. Maybe you want to be a business owner, which also requires a completely different skill set. Not only do you have to be a good manager and good at sales, but you also have to learn about actually operating a business.

> **As you progress in a trades career with an open mind and a willingness to learn, you will find out that your trade goes way beyond just turning a wrench.**

The tradesperson who embraces *a mindset of lifelong learning* will never get stuck. They will always learn what they need to learn when it's time to learn it—what's known as "just-in-time learning." They could even enroll in a college degree program once they're a little older and know themselves better.

Ryan Gorman, the former CEO of Coldwell Banker, agrees. He puts it this way:

> *Hopefully, the mid-career college experience will become acceptable at some point so that when kids turn eighteen,*

parents don't have to make the choice of whether to encourage or discourage one thing or another but rather to equip the kids for life. We should make sure they have a longer perspective, a longer time horizon, and permission to think, "Ten years from now, I can change my mind. There are a lot of options for me."

I've got a few more arguments for why those working in the skilled trades are unstuckable. Many skilled trades show promising (if not astronomical) projected growth, especially in expanding industries. For example, industrial machinery mechanic jobs are projected to increase more rapidly than industrial engineering jobs. And as we use more renewable energy and require skilled tradespeople to install and maintain those energy sources, we can expect job growth to explode.

Take wind turbine technician jobs, for instance. They are expected to increase a whopping 68% by 2030! There has never been a better time to get into the trades. Our society has a shortage of skilled workers, and that shortage is only going to expand with all the Baby Boomers aging out of the job market. The demand for skilled workers is far bigger than the supply.

Perhaps you worry that some skilled trades may be slated for automation, especially those that deal with machinery, as we saw in the 2005 film *Charlie and the Chocolate Factory* starring Johnny Depp. (I prefer the 1971 version, *Willy Wonka and the Chocolate Factory,* myself. Gene Wilder was charming as Willy Wonka. You could tell he had the whole thing under control the entire time. On the other hand, Depp's portrayal of Wonka was more of an out-of-control, deeply disturbed character. The whole

> **The demand for skilled workers is far bigger than the supply.**

thing felt more like a creepy fever dream than a whimsical character lesson. But I digress.)

In the 2005 version of the movie, Mr. Bucket gets laid off from capping toothpaste tubes because a robot could do his job.

Spoiler alert: Mr. Bucket gets a better-paying job as a repair technician for the machines that took his first job.

Unlike some unskilled jobs, skilled craftsmanship relies on human artistry and many areas of intelligence. The jobs that are most likely to be automated don't require troubleshooting, craftsmanship, or physically getting into hard-to-reach places to repair something. Many trades need us to see, hear, feel, and even sniff out issues with machinery, building materials, and more. While robots can detect and troubleshoot problems they have been programmed to fix, they don't have senses that are as diverse and adaptable as ours. The odds are good that most skilled trades aren't going anywhere anytime soon.

Here's another argument for why the skilled trades are unstuckable. Think back to when the COVID-19 pandemic hit. Many people were furloughed and couldn't make money due to lockdowns and business closures. However, a certain class of workers kept working and earning their wages because they were deemed essential.

Who fell into that category?

The obvious answers are nurses, doctors, and grocery store clerks. We saw those folks on the news or every time we needed to buy food for the week. But who else worked during the pandemic? HVAC technicians, electricians, machinery repairers, and many other tradespeople.

When the whole world pauses, AC units, cars, and electronics don't get the memo. Appliances still break down, and someone needs to be out there troubleshooting and doing repairs. Windows break, airplane engines need servicing, horses need their hooves trimmed, and the list goes on. Meanwhile, court cases stall, bars and restaurants close, and other workplaces shut down during public crises. However, the skilled workers continue to bring home the bacon. Tradespeople are less likely to have to worry about feeding their family during a public crisis with widespread furloughs.

Now, let's get down to the nitty-gritty: pay. Are people going to get rich automatically by working in the skilled trades? No. Can they earn a solid living? Absolutely—and becoming wealthy isn't out of the question, either.

> **The opportunity to use the trades as a springboard to higher-compensating jobs—and even becoming a business owner—is a reality.**

According to the U.S. Bureau of Labor Statistics, the 2020 median annual pay for an HVACR technician or installer was well above the national median, as was the median annual pay for an automotive service technician. Installers and repairers of power lines and fiber optics made nearly double the national median—without any postsecondary education requirements. Many jobs that require a university degree don't pay anywhere close to that. And the salaries are projected to rise even higher.

People can earn a decent living working in the skilled trades without losing chunks of their wages to student loan payments each month. Keep in mind, too, that the opportunity to use the trades as a springboard to higher-compensating jobs—and even becoming a business owner—is a reality.

Skilled tradespeople can also save money on repairs and DIY projects around their homes. They also often help out family members and friends who find themselves in sticky, expensive situations with their homes. Do they *have* to do their work for free? Absolutely not—I won't stop anybody from charging their in-laws the full price of a repair if they want to. But it can feel nice to help out Grandma, who doesn't know anything about her car, or lend a hand to the best man at your wedding if his AC quits working in the dead of summer. How satisfying would that be?

So, let's recap. The skilled trades offer:

- immense flexibility
- the potential for career advancement
- excellent job-growth outlook
- no student loan debt
- above-average pay
- essential work that truly helps people
- enhanced self-sufficiency
- the opportunity to be *the* revered go-to guy or gal in the family and neighborhood

I don't know about you, but that doesn't sound like the definition of *stuck* to me. It sounds more like the definition of *freedom*.

6 Raising Autodidacts

Ask any six-year-old kid if they know how to use an iPhone or a tablet. Go ahead—I'll wait.

Of course, they do. Their little fingers can swipe through screens, open and close apps, and search YouTube for their favorite Nerf battle video faster than you can say, "Too much screen time!" In all likelihood, they could deftly navigate a mobile device before they could read or write. Even more likely, a mobile device had a big part in their *learning* to read and write.

How did they learn to use an iPhone at such a young age? Well, they messed around with it until they figured it out. Nobody taught them how to use that device. They taught themselves. It's like learning to ride a bike. Sure, we might hold the kid steady for a minute, but they teach themselves how to balance, pedal, steer, and—hopefully—stop. Their natural inclinations and desire to learn are what guide them. The same is true of a child learning to walk or speak their native tongue. In the words of those great philosophers from the Nike® advertising team, they Just Do It. Naturally.

> **Kids are natural autodidacts.**

Imagine what would happen if, before allowing the six-year-old child to try and ride the shiny new bike you just gave them for their birthday, you made them sit down at a desk and listen to a three-hour presentation on gears and how they work, tires and how they're made, why the wheels have spokes, and Newton's Laws of Motion (specifically the Second Law of Motion dealing with acceleration) and… ugh.

Major yawner. Epic fail. The poor kid just wants to climb on the bike and go! If you start by letting the child ride the bike, they will be excited and probably super curious about how it works. *Then* you can help them learn about gears and tires and Newton.

That's because kids are natural *autodidacts*. (I love the word autodidact. Say it five times fast, just for fun. I always do.) An **autodidact** is a person who is self-taught—in other words, a self-learner. They don't learn their skills through formal education. They teach themselves, relying on any material and tools they can get their hands on. Unsurprisingly, many autodidacts are avid readers or tinkerers.

In the HVACR trade, the autodidact is the technician who reads every manual and studies the schematics to gain a fundamental understanding of wiring and systems. Another autodidactic technician may have never learned how to cut and shape sheet metal in trade school, so they buy sheet metal, tools, and books and learn how to do it themselves.

No matter their profession, autodidacts are the best troubleshooters because they constantly expand their stockpile of knowledge, and they enjoy doing it. They will be top performers wherever they choose to work because their lifelong desire to learn and improve will always keep them at the top of their game.

Many prominent historical figures fall under the autodidact category. There's Leonardo da Vinci, who painted the most famous painting of all time and was a biomechanic before it was cool (or even a real thing). Da

Vinci's family noticed his artistic talent early on, so they neglected his formal education in favor of an art apprenticeship.

Although da Vinci was best known for his art, he also made incredible discoveries in human anatomy and physiology despite lacking formal education in Latin and mathematics. He taught himself Latin and used his other skills to learn how the human body's functions relate to its form. Da Vinci took an observational approach to science. He watched the human body in motion and examined cadavers to make his discoveries in biomechanics well before biomechanics became a known area of study.

Da Vinci's conclusions called some established medical principles into question. For example, during his time, scientists and scholars believed that the liver was the central organ controlling blood in the body. Through his observations and constructions of organ models, da Vinci discovered that it was actually the heart.

And how about Benjamin Franklin? In addition to being one of America's Founding Fathers, he was a prolific inventor. He created the lightning rod and bifocal glasses and made some key observations about cooling (a personal favorite of mine). He conducted experiments with his friend, Cambridge University professor John Hadley, on the evaporation of volatile liquids like ether and alcohol. Franklin and Hadley discovered that evaporating these liquids could rapidly cool down an object, laying the foundation for future developments in refrigeration and air conditioning.

Franklin was a brilliant man. He was an enthusiastic reader from the time he was a young child. As an adult, he joined a group of like-minded artisans and tradesmen who focused on self-improvement. Books were expensive at the time, so he suggested that the group pool their resources to purchase books and run a subscription library, an uncommon idea in the colonies. That way, all the self-learners in the group had access to a collection of educational resources.

Surely, you must be thinking, *intellectuals of da Vinci's and Franklin's caliber owe their brilliance to extensive schooling*. Nope! In fact, neither of them had a complete formal education. It made no difference. Everything they learned and everything that contributed to their success was fueled by their determination and love of self-directed learning.

But their stories don't exactly fit the context of the world where we live and work today. What about modern autodidacts? Many self-learners today are highly successful people who are masters of their craft. Do the names Steve Jobs and James Cameron ring any bells?

Steve Jobs founded Apple, one of the world's largest and most successful technology companies. I'm willing to bet that right now, some of you are reading this book on an iPhone, iPad, or MacBook, or you ordered it on one. If so, you (and I!) have Steve Jobs to thank. We all have some idea about the scope of his work. It's pretty impressive.

You might think that Jobs received his foundation from a college degree in engineering or at least went to business school, but the truth is that he had no degree in anything. He enrolled at Reed College in Portland, Oregon, in 1972 and dropped out after six months for financial reasons. However, he continued to attend classes informally for another eighteen months. Jobs honed most of his technological skills by tinkering in his garage (though much credit also goes to his friend Steve Wozniak). That garage was the birthplace of the very first Apple computer, and it was not the fruit of formal education.

Schooling, or lack thereof, did not dictate their lives. Instead, their love of learning and problem-solving did.

James Cameron is another example. You probably know him as the Academy Award-winning director of such blockbuster movies as *Titanic, Ava-*

tar, *Aliens,* and *Terminator*. What I find most impressive is that he is a college dropout who is entirely self-taught in filmmaking. He learned in his spare time while working odd jobs, including truck driving and being a janitor. Cameron perfected his craft based purely on his own grit and love for learning.

But Cameron didn't limit his self-learning to making movies. He also helped NASA develop cameras for the Mars Rover and co-designed a submersible vehicle for deep sea exploration, which he personally test-piloted, setting a record for diving five miles beneath the surface of the Pacific Ocean solo. Again, it was all done through self-directed learning.

Now it's time to tell the story of someone *with* a degree who took his passion even further—much further. Remember the airplane my grandfather built from a kit, the Long-EZ? It was designed by aerospace engineer Burt Rutan, who managed to change the world of aviation and space travel forever.

Born in 1943 in Oregon (the same year as my Grandpa), Rutan grew up with a passion for airplanes. He built model planes as a child, and this fascination with aviation grew stronger as he got older. After earning a degree in aeronautical engineering from California Polytechnic State University (Cal Tech), Rutan started his career at Edwards Air Force Base as a flight test engineer. But it was his innate curiosity and self-learning abilities that propelled him to new heights.

Although Rutan had formal training in aeronautical engineering, much of his groundbreaking work can be attributed to his autodidactic nature. He didn't rely solely on what he learned in school; instead, he was driven to explore, experiment, and learn independently. This curiosity and thirst for knowledge helped him develop innovative designs that challenged conventional wisdom in the aerospace industry.

One of Rutan's most famous creations was the Voyager aircraft, which another aviator piloted for the first non-stop, unrefueled flight around the world in 1986. The Voyager was unique, as it was built using lightweight materials and an unconventional design that enabled it to fly long distances without refueling. This accomplishment was made possible by Rutan's willingness to think outside the box and his dedication to learning through hands-on experience.

Rutan's self-taught expertise also played a significant role in developing SpaceShipOne, the world's first privately funded manned spacecraft. In 2004, SpaceShipOne made history by reaching the edge of space and safely returning to Earth. This achievement earned Rutan the prestigious Ansari X Prize and paved the way for a new era of commercial space travel.

Sure, these are cool stories, but how do they relate to educating our kids? Well, you've probably noticed that all the above people lacked or had an incomplete formal education in one or multiple fields that they revolutionized—and they chose to develop certain skills on their own.

Schooling, or lack thereof, did not dictate their lives. Instead, their love of learning and problem-solving did, and it stamped them as extraordinary individuals. They had the core traits of autodidacts and changed the world, guided merely by their inner nerdiness and desire to learn and understand.

You might be wondering what da Vinci, Franklin, Jobs, Cameron, and Rutan have to do with that six-year-old kid of yours who is probably (hopefully) making a big batch of mud pies in your flower garden right now. I know it's a challenge sometimes, but I want you to look for the autodidact in that kid and nurture the heck out of your child. It's in there, I promise you. You might have to tease it out, but it will be worth it because, as our previously-mentioned autodidacts have proven, some of the most useful and powerful learning comes not from formal education but from our own curiosity and determination to know.

You can support the autodidact that already exists in your children in a few ways. First, catch them doing something they're interested in or having fun with. Then, guide them toward learning more about it.

For example, go to the kid making mud pies in your garden and say, "Hey, I've always wondered where dirt comes from—like, what's it made of? Do you know?"

The little scientist may stop mid-mud pie and shake their head in curiosity.

"Hmmm," you say. "I wonder where we could find out?"

And BOOM! You're off to the autodidact races as your child begins finding out whatever they can about dirt.

This technique goes way beyond mud pies. You can use it for anything they show an interest in. Encourage them to layer some knowledge upon the joy they're experiencing doing whatever it might be: fishing, cooking, skipping rope, drawing, dancing, or building with Legos, for instance. Give them opportunities to discover how much fun it is to dig deeper (mud pie reference intended).

The most powerful way to excite your children about the beauty and value of self-directed learning is to model it yourself.

Next, introduce your kids, literally and figuratively, to autodidacts from all walks of life. Talk to them about famous self-learners like da Vinci, Franklin, Jobs, Cameron, George Washington Carver, Louisa May Alcott, the Wright Brothers, Louis L'Amour, Frederick Douglass, Frida Kahlo, David Bowie, Maya Angelou, and Frank Lloyd Wright, among many others.

Also, tell them about the not-so-famous autodidacts—say, your neighbor who taught herself to play piano as a child and now gives lessons to all the kids in town or the young couple with a booth at the farmer's market who taught themselves beekeeping and now have a flourishing honey business, and so on.

If your family is anything like mine, you have a goldmine of inspiring ancestry to pull from, too—you'll probably find multiple autodidacts in your family tree with a little more climbing up the branches. It doesn't matter if they're not glamorous. Celebrate and elevate them anyway.

But the most powerful way to excite your children about the beauty and value of self-directed learning is to model it yourself. When they see you joyfully dedicating your time and energy to learning new things—whether for some practical application or simply for fun—they will remember and follow you. It won't matter if they ultimately choose a path of higher education or take a different road. They will become autodidacts who take responsibility for their own learning. Like the horse that knows where to find the water, they won't have to wait for someone to lead them when they start to feel a little thirsty. They will have free rein to go there on their own.

During a Q&A session after one of my presentations on alternatives to college, a woman stood up and told me a story. She was a teacher with multiple college degrees, and she had a sixteen-year-old son with mild dyslexia and ADHD on the gifted spectrum.

"He can fix anything," she said. "It's just wacky to me, all the crazy things he can do. He figured out how to launch his own LLC, so he has his own business. He started out mowing yards, but now he's into landscape design because our neighbor does landscape design, and he thinks it's cool. He also volunteers at the airport because he's fascinated with avionics."

"The other day," she continued, "our air conditioner stopped working, and we were freaking out about the money. Two hours later, our son comes in and tells us what we need to do to fix it. I was, like: How do you know this? And he said, 'I YouTube *everything*, Mom.' So my question is: How do you temper a child who is trying to do everything at once? How do you get him to settle down and focus?"

My answer to her (and other parents with similar stories): You *don't* temper that child. You let them do it *all*. He is already doing exactly what he needs: exploring, learning, and building his skills portfolio. So encourage this young autodidact. Let him run, and don't worry about where he'll be when he's eighteen or nineteen. He'll probably do thirty more crazy things, but by the time he's twenty-five, he might be a billionaire or, better yet, a generous giver. Be thankful he isn't on his phone worrying about being accepted by his peers.

7 Apprenticeship and Mentorship

Parents often ask me at what age kids should start pursuing their interests and exploring careers. My advice? Probably not before the age of three since they need to be eating solid food first. It makes packing the lunch box a lot easier!

But seriously, as a society, we must open our minds and allow our children to branch out and discover all the learning and career opportunities available to them rather than automatically funneling them down the prescribed educational path. We shouldn't be afraid to expose them to alternatives.

As a society, we must open our minds and allow our children to branch out and discover all the learning and career opportunities available to them.

I say "afraid" because I see how fear prevents many parents from giving their kids even a glimpse of the possibilities for their future. They're afraid the kids might pick something that's not law, engineering, or medicine. If that describes you, please set those fears aside and let your kids have new and varied experiences! It will enrich their lives.

I can recommend a couple of ways you can go about finding your kids (or yourself) these exploration opportunities: **mentorship** and **apprenticeship**. We don't hear much about good old-fashioned mentorships and apprenticeships these days. That's because they are more informal, fluid ways of learning, and our educational system has become very highly structured.

The rationale for creating a structured educational system (and structured society) goes back to our manufacturing-based past. Factory owners needed workers who could do what robots do today: repetitive manual labor, day in and day out. Workers were generally okay with that. You packed your lunch, punched the clock, did your thing, punched the clock again, cashed your paycheck, went bowling with your friends—and at the end of it all, you collected your pension. That was your life, and in the shadow of the World Wars and the Great Depression, it made a lot of sense for you and your employer to want it that way.

But that's not where we're at right now, soon to enter the second quarter of the 21st century. Yes, there's an effort to rebuild our manufacturing capabilities in America—but even if we do, technology and robotics are going to do much of the work.

So what type of employees do today's employers really want? We want **problem solvers**. Apprenticeships and mentorships are about creating problem solvers and letting young workers meet and learn from people who are not only skilled but also passionate about their work.

First up is mentorship. Mentorship is one-to-one guidance and nurturing, and unfortunately, it's lacking in today's society. I was blessed to have multiple mentors: my dad, my mom, my grandpa, my uncle. I already told you how my grandpa put me to work at his aircraft salvage yard. My uncle also became my mentor when I was fourteen. He had me working in grocery stores: hanging lighting and pushing a scaffold around. That's patently in opposition to labor laws, and I don't recommend it, but my family has a long history of illegal child labor. I was just carrying on the tradition.

As an HVAC professional, I had my kids riding along with me and using my tools when they were eight or nine years old. That was not because I intended for them to become air conditioning techs. It was because I wanted to spend time with them and allow them to learn why we're not all melting in our homes and offices during the summer, why we can ship produce around the world and have it arrive fresh—basically, how the entire economy runs. I love mentoring my kids this way, and they get a kick out of it, too. Admittedly, they got more of a kick out of it when they were little. By the time they were thirteen, they were rolling their eyes.

> **Mentorship is best if that mentor is not you, the parent—especially when your kids become teenagers.**

Mentorship is best if that mentor is not you, the parent—especially when your kids become teenagers. If you have teenagers, you know what I'm talking about because there's nobody stupider than Mom and Dad for a while in the mind of a teen. So look for a mentor who is not you: Find a person who is doing something your kids think is interesting and who will report back to you and keep you informed.

The best teacher-mentors are not necessarily the smartest or most experienced. They are the best because they are passionate about what they do and are excited to share it. So when seeking a mentor for your kids or yourself, look for that passion. Look for a lifelong learner who gets excited when they are proven wrong rather than taking it as a giant ego hit. That's one of the primary distinctions between a person who is a lifelong learner and one who isn't: lifelong learners don't mind finding out that they are wrong.

In addition to mentorship is apprenticeship. "Apprenticeship" is a word I want us to use more often, but I want to see it used in a new way. For millennia, apprenticeship meant you worked alongside someone (or a system of someones) to gain the necessary skills to do a specific vocation well. Recently, it's become associated with unions and the government. I'm not saying there's anything wrong with that, but we don't always need that centralized structure to make an apprenticeship work. We need systems where people can gain exposure and experience; that exposure shouldn't be limited to learning about typical jobs and trades. It could also include the arts, such as culinary arts, music, publishing, crafts, media, graphic arts, game design, and more.

> **Immersion is always the best teacher.**

It's not enough just to read and watch documentaries about those kinds of vocations and avocations. If you want to understand something, do you think you would understand it best by reading about it, watching it on a screen, or experiencing it? Immersion is always the best teacher.

Think about the conventional way of learning a foreign language; we take Italian for a couple of years in high school and come away with very little to show for it. We've learned *about* the language but not how to speak it fluently. But if you were to experience Italian immersively and know that you couldn't get your next meal or learn where the bathroom was until you asked for it in Italian, you would learn Italian quickly.

That's what apprenticeship does. It isn't any more complicated than that. Every type of work that exists in the world has some form of apprenticeship. There just probably isn't a government program for it. (Thank heavens.)

Apprentice options include **registered apprenticeships**, which can be union or non-union and are run through the U.S. Department of Labor. The

Florida Department of Education has programs called **pre-apprenticeships** for youth aged 16 to 18 who want to experience different jobs. Some of them are in the trades, while some of them aren't. Then there's **on-the-job training**, which can be good or not so good, depending on the strength of whoever is doing the training.

A young person can also arrange to do short-term (one-to-three-month) **internships**, which are available in a wide range of occupational niches. Many college degree programs now require students to complete an internship towards the end of their education to apply their classroom skills in real-world situations. Internships can be paid or unpaid.

While academic internships generally require a student to be enrolled in a college or university, other types of internships do not. A young person could approach an employer and work with them to arrange an internship to get on-the-job experience to see if an occupation feels like a good career fit for them.

Finally, we have **private apprenticeships**, which is what I've been driving towards over the last twenty years. Private apprenticeships take place outside the school system and with minimal to no government involvement, meaning there's less chance for bureaucracy and waste. (Depending on where you are in the country, private programs may not be able to call themselves "apprenticeships" unless they are registered and may go by a different name.)

Regardless of what we call them, I am advocating for the ability to create apprenticeship programs and opportunities for young people, even if the official structure or the institutional backing isn't necessarily there. I want to see mass participation in apprenticeship wherever possible by any sort of trade that requires skilled workers. I started that sort of private apprenticeship program for a large local company before I co-founded my own company, where I've run private apprenticeships for many years. They provide a great way for people to gain experience and perspective.

Many rewarding professions that offer apprenticeships and don't require a college degree are out there in professions like electric work, plumbing, HVAC, construction, culinary arts, and so many more.

Let's say your kid spends a couple of years going through an apprenticeship in one of these trades and comes out disliking the profession and not wanting to continue. Are they stuck? No, not at all. Your young person can do whatever they want now, including going to college. After all, they just (hopefully) made money on their apprenticeship and also learned something valuable for their future. If they saved their money, they could pay their college tuition in cash.

8 Experience Before Lecture

It's summertime, and you've decided to teach your five-year-old daughter about the life cycle of the monarch butterfly. Super interesting stuff for kids of all ages, right? So you sit her down and explain that the female butterfly lays eggs on a milkweed plant, and then the eggs hatch into caterpillars. Then the caterpillars eat the milkweed, and then, one day, the caterpillar forms a chrysalis—and a couple of weeks later, an adult butterfly emerges.

This lesson makes perfect sense to you, but here's what your five-year-old is picturing in her mind as you spin this magical yarn:

- A butterfly lays eggs (like the ones you cracked open for her breakfast this morning?)
- The eggs land on a milkweed plant (milk, like the yummy drink she enjoyed with said breakfast? She thought milk came from cows, not weeds!)
- The eggs hatch (like baby chicks?), and out pops a caterpillar who makes a chrysalis (what in the world is THAT, Dad?)
- And eventually there's a metamorphosis (met-a-porpoises—what?) that turns that caterpillar into a butterfly inside the chrysalis (yawn …)

But what if, instead of just telling your child about this phenomenon of nature, the two of you head outside and find some milkweed? Together, you pinch off a piece of a leaf so she can see the white milky liquid that comes out, which explains the origin of the plant's name. The two of you then nurture the milkweed and wait for the inevitable arrival of a monarch. A monarch comes by and lays her eggs on the leaves, and you hand your child a magnifying glass so that she can see that they're nothing like the eggs she eats for breakfast. She learns that there are all kinds of eggs in the animal world.

> **We have to experience things before we can understand the lecture.**

When the caterpillars hatch, you watch them devour the milkweed leaves and grow bigger and bigger until, one day, you find a chrysalis hanging near the plant. You explain how the caterpillar made the chrysalis and how it will protect the insect while it's changing into a butterfly. You count the days until the monarch finally emerges, pumps up its wings, and flies away to make more eggs, caterpillars, chrysalises, and butterflies.

Now your child has context for the metamorphosis lecture to come! Now she can focus on learning more about the process because the words will make sense.

We have to experience things before we can understand the lecture. Somebody can tell you the definition of "chrysalis," but if you don't have subjective experience with the word, it's difficult to understand what it really means.

Language relies on mental models that are based on experience. That's how we learn to speak. It's how we learn to read or to ride a bike. We experience something and then develop mental models. Then, somebody tells us what those experiences are called and what those words mean.

When learning a new skill, there is simply no substitute for having a chance to use all of our senses in the real world, in context.

So if that's true (and it definitely is), why is it that in our standard educational system, we tend to use words and books and photos to teach rather than actual tactile experiences? I can tell you why—because it's easier and more convenient to lecture than to provide real hands-on experience.

Another excuse for not providing students with experiential learning opportunities is that it's "safer" to teach them in a classroom—although I think risk tends to be overstated in modern society. Somebody smashing a thumb or getting a bloody nose isn't the end of the world.

But it's really not about trying to prevent kids from getting badly hurt. It's about trying to prevent inconvenience. We're trying to manufacture the inconvenience out of the education process. I think that's a mistake.

I advocate designing systems where the experience comes before the bookwork because the bookwork or the lectures will make a lot more sense. When you've already seen something—even if you didn't fully understand what you saw—you will remember. The experience will give you a foundation upon which to start building knowledge. Then, when you see a PowerPoint slide during a lecture, you'll recall your previous experience, and the slide will mean something to you. It's that interface between experience and language bouncing back and forth that helps contextualize the education.

Somebody smashing a thumb or getting a bloody nose isn't the end of the world.

That's why apprenticeship and mentorship are so effective, by the way. So seek out opportunities to gain hands-on experiences for yourself and your kids, then observe the educational metamorphoses that follow.

9 Repz Make Gainz

I have a confession: Workout bros and jocks annoy me. They really do. They're so competitive, flexing their muscles and showing off their physical skills all the time. That irritates me. But to be honest, it's probably not them—it's me.

I am kind of bitter that I'm not a more talented athlete. The fact that my dad was an exceptional college football standout doesn't help. I didn't inherit his aptitude in that regard, and it bugged me a little when I was younger. And then what did I do? I married into an athletic family. So I'm surrounded by all these physically gifted people (at least in comparison to me).

Repetition doesn't feel natural for me— or at least that was the excuse I tried on for size.

I was even more surrounded when I joined a gym and started doing CrossFit after my friend Matt scammed me into it. It wasn't easy for me—not because I couldn't do the workout (which I often couldn't) but because I found it boring. The trainers kept saying, "Reps make gains! Reps make gains!" as they tried to get me to push myself harder. I found that totally uninspiring. Doing the same thing over and over again was flat-out tedious.

Some people are inherently able to do massive reps without boredom, but I'm an autodidact, a self-learner. Repetition doesn't feel natural for me—or at least that was the excuse I tried on for size.

But I stuck with the CrossFit thing, and the more I did it, the more I realized that the trainers were right. Reps really do lead to gains. Practice really does make perfect. When you do the same thing over and over again and measure your proficiency at regular intervals, you see qualitative or quantitative improvement—or usually both. If you don't give up, you'll see that your reps become faster (quantitative gain), but you also get to the point where you understand the technique better and like it more (qualitative gain).

The "reps make gains" concept translates into just about anything we do. The reason why I was able to become a competent air conditioning technician is because I fixed thousands of air conditioners. I replaced hundreds of compressors and expansion valves and did thousands of startups on new equipment and many, many installs myself (many of them done terribly, I must confess). I applied Malcolm Gladwell's famous 10,000-hour rule, which he claims is necessary for developing mastery or expertise in a skill area.

All those repetitive experiences—whether I did a good job or a bad job, whether I was successful or a failure, whether I made money or didn't make money—built those muscles and my ability to grow in that context.

Not only did I learn a lot of efficiencies through that experience of repetition and mastery, but it also exposed me to a lot of different variables in small, manageable amounts. I wasn't facing complete chaos each time. That's a good thing, and in fact, it's often what traditional educational models try to do. They try to loop students back around to build on things they already know. But the problem is that they don't always give them the tactile experience. They tend to stack knowledge on top of knowledge rather than stacking reps on top of reps (aka "actually doing stuff") as a means of mastery. That's when those *Eureka!* moments can happen since you're focused enough to recognize them when they float up.

In anything we do, we have to have significant repetition, but we improve the quality and quantity of those repetitions as we gain varied experiences associated with them. When parents pressure their kids to specialize in certain sports too young, it actually hinders their progress compared to kids who gain exposure to a wide range of different experiences. That exposure gives them a broader sense of muscle dexterity so that they make bigger gains when they do the reps.

This whole idea reminds me of the Wright Brothers. Orville and Wilbur started out making bicycles and had some decent luck with that, but their real passion was flight. They tried many, many different things before they had success. One of the major challenges they faced was that the existing lift model that scientists believed to be true, specifically as related to the curve of the wing, just wasn't working. No matter how many times they tried to get the craft airborne, it failed.

Many people practice a bored, somewhat impatient version of entrepreneurism.

After much trial and error, the Wright Brothers figured out that the angle of attack had more to do with lift than the curve of the wing did. Obviously, both had an impact, but it was the attack angle that mattered more. Had the brothers not done those reps patiently, painstakingly, and repeatedly, they would never have made that gain–an entrepreneurial discovery that changed the world.

Many people practice a bored, somewhat impatient version of entrepreneurism. You know—throw any old idea at the wall, see if it sticks, and if it doesn't work out right away, move on to the next shiny object.

But that's not at all what I'm advocating. I'm advocating for the kind of shotgun approach where you explore ideas but also take the time to develop skills along the way. Then, once you find a problem worth solving, dive in and do your reps until you figure it out and master it. Not only will the problem be solved, but you will also emerge as a stronger, more well-rounded person.

It's like doing CrossFit minus the forced proximity to workout bros. Sign me up!

10 Don't Take Me to Lunch

As Will Farrell's character Ron Burgundy famously said in the movie *Anchorman*, "I don't know how to put this, but I'm kind of a big deal." Sometimes, I say this line as an obvious joke.

Let me clarify. I *am not* "kind of a big deal." I co-own a business and teach HVAC. That's all. Outside of work, I am not a big deal *at all*. At home, I'm just that guy wandering around the house looking confused. Getting in the way. Tripping over the pile of laundry. Searching in vain for the stash of candy bars I hid from the children. Trying to identify the source of that weird odor in the hallway that my wife can smell but I can't. You know, that guy. The Dad.

But when I go back to the office on Monday morning, salespeople are in line trying to get face time with me. They usually start their sales pitch by asking if they can take me to lunch. Their goal is to build a relationship with me, but not because they want to connect on a human level, challenge my way of thinking, or add value to my life. Nor do they hope that I will do those things for them.

They want to connect with me strictly so that I will buy whatever they're selling. End of story.

I like a free meal as much as the next guy, but I'm not going to play games in order to get it. (That is, unless the game is *Risk*. I will beat you at *Risk* and then happily eat that free food.)

Unfortunately, our society is built on making social connections with people we really don't want to spend time with. We force ourselves into those spaces and then wonder why so many of our relationships are shallow and transactional.

In their excellent book *The Challenger Sale: Taking Control of the Customer Conversation*, authors Matthew Dixon and Brent Adamson dispute traditional sales techniques and provide a new approach to selling. In a nutshell, *The Challenger Sale* promotes the idea that being a great salesperson isn't about just building relationships and taking people to lunch. Instead, it's about challenging the customer's thinking, providing valuable insights, and guiding them toward a decision that benefits them. By adopting this approach, salespeople can create more value for their customers and, ultimately, be more successful in their sales careers.

> **Unfortunately, our society is built on making social connections with people we really don't want to spend time with.**

Here's what this means for those of us who hope to guide more people toward a rewarding career: Many of the most talented communicators in our society—the people who most naturally connect with others—fall into the easiest possible career path for themselves, which is often sales. And many of them see the best version of sales as relationship selling, especially if they're really good at establishing rapport and persuading people to buy what they're selling.

I've seen this happen a lot in the homeschooling community with bright kids who can talk a good game. I think pursuing this path is often a mistake for the talented communicator because it can easily lack substance—they end up selling themselves short.

The most impactful sellers—the entrepreneurial-minded or challenger sellers, people who could actually run a business and continue to grow and do things they're really proud of—can take the skills that make them good salespeople and apply them to something bigger. They can apply that autodidactic talent to deeply understanding a problem that needs solving—and then building an amazing career on that. When you develop expertise, you become more than just a likable person to buy from. You become a valuable resource.

I think back to the times I watched my grandfather shoot the breeze with his customers in his office. The context for those relationships was not just about talk and banter. Papa was an expert on aircraft—and aircraft parts. His expertise led to a relationship with his customers that was substantive. It was deeper and more meaningful than the simple transactional nature of most sales relationships because he helped them, and they helped him. Their relationship had cross-benefits. Given a choice between buying a part from the guy who could talk your ear off about the ball game or buying a part from my grandfather who could spin a yarn but was also an expert on salvaged aircraft parts, the customers would pick my grandfather every time.

This model is a much healthier way of doing business and is the way of the future. The salespeople who figure this out will not be stopped. They will never be stuck because they have the mental capacity and flexibility to learn whatever they need to learn in order to serve their clients. And that's what it's all about.

11 Head Cartoons

If you needed to teach a young child about levers, how would you start the lesson? How would you even begin to describe this vital aspect of physics? I asked a group of homeschooling parents this question at a family education conference, and the answers I received were enlightening.

"Basically, you have a pivot point on something straight and utilize weight on both sides to figure out where the balance point is," said one parent.

"Pivot point, weight, balance point," I replied, nodding. "I like it! Anyone else?"

"A lever is the use of distribution of energy to accomplish a means," said another.

"Distribution of energy to accomplish a means," I repeated. "Great! Anyone else?"

A woman in the back of the room raised her hand and said, "I'd tell the child to picture a seesaw…"

BINGO! That's what I'm talking about! If you want to teach a kid something new, *start with something they already know*. This teaching method helps the child construct a mental model (or brain model) that they can build upon as they learn more. My brother and I call this "the cartoon in my head," which really helps with problem-solving in our line of work.

Our dad, who was an electrician back in the day, used brain models, too, as he approached the job of fixing electrical systems lying behind walls. He couldn't see what was back there, but he had to start somewhere, so he created a mental model of electricity that involved visualizing wires as pipes carrying water. He taught me about voltage, amperage, and resistance using this head cartoon when I was little. It always stuck with me.

I think the reason so many kids struggle to learn is that they haven't been taught about the cartoon in their head and how helpful it can be. Once they comprehend what cartoons are and understand that they already know how to create and build upon them, they can use them to their advantage as life-long learners. You should probably explain that their cartoon may or may not look like a SpongeBob episode. That's up to them. Mine often have something to do with He-Man because I was a little kid in the early 80s. Don't judge me.

Every time a child grasps something—really grasps it—I can guarantee you they have established a mental model. Now, that mental model may not be perfect (just like electricity as water), but it will be effective in helping them take the next step. I can't stress this point enough—never discourage kids (or anyone else) from using an imperfect model when they're learning if it brings them to the next step. You can always address the misunderstanding later, but let them run with it for now.

> **I think the reason so many kids struggle to learn is that they haven't been taught about the cartoon in their head and how helpful it can be.**

I have a great example of this. At the same home education convention where I asked the audience about levers, my family set up a booth with an interactive display where kids could tinker around with electrical circuits and build some things. One afternoon, a little boy stepped up to the display. I could see the gears turning in his mind as he looked at it and wondered how this thing worked. I could tell he was really smart. He was definitely curious.

I handed him a little wire connector with an alligator clip, the kind partially covered in a rubber sleeve. (You've probably seen such an alligator clip and can picture exactly what I'm talking about. If not, Google it and then come back.)

So the little boy grabbed the clip and turned it over and around in his hands, trying to figure out how to get the jaws open. He tried to pry it open from the front because, in his mind, that was how it should have worked. Of course, it didn't. As he fiddled around with the clip, I just sat back and watched him. I didn't say a word. He continued for a few minutes until he eventually pulled back the little rubber sleeve giving him access to the spring-loaded end. He pinched it, the clip opened, and he was grinning from ear to ear.

Now, here's what usually happens in situations like this—we discount that fumbling, bumbling process of discovery. We want to jump in and say, "Oh, no, no, do it like this!" We want to make it easy for the child. But guess what? That little guy is always going to remember how alligator clips work now. He started with what he already had, his tactile skill, and figured it out himself. Now he's got a cartoon in his head that he can build knowledge upon for the rest of his life.

And who knows how far that might take him?

12 Curiosity and Mastery

One day, when I was driving along, minding my own business, listening to some nerdy podcast as usual, I saw a strange bird standing in a swampy ditch on the side of the road. I'd never seen anything like it. It was about the size of an egret, but instead of being white, as egrets are, it was brown and dappled with white spots. This bird had a long, curved bill similar to another common local bird called an ibis. Still, having lived in Florida my entire life, I knew it was neither an egret nor an ibis.

I decided that when I got home, I'd try to find it in one of our bird identification books or on a birding app. Meanwhile, as I drove along, I kept thinking about that bird and then birds in general.

Hmm, I wonder what kind of bird that was? I mused. *I wonder how many different species of birds there are in Florida. I wonder how many there are in the world?*

At home, I looked up that weird bird. Turns out it was a limpkin (*Aramus guarauna*). Limpkins are monotypic, meaning they are their family's only members (*Aramidae*). They live in freshwater marshes and eat mostly apple snails. According to the website, limpkins have a "haunting cry" that they perform primarily at night. I also learned that there are 936 species of birds in Florida and as many as 18,000 species worldwide.

And then, I closed the web page and went on with my life.

The way I see it, there are two kinds of curiosity. The first leads to the accumulation of knowledge that some might call "useless" (and while I don't believe that any knowledge can really be considered useless, the stuff I learned about the limpkin comes mighty close), which is superficial, trivial knowledge that you collect but never really apply in your life unless you're a contestant on *Jeopardy!* Many people have this type of boundless curiosity. It comes naturally to them to want to know more. They can't help but wonder.

The second type of curiosity extends beyond simply wondering. Rather than being endlessly curious about the surface of things, you desire to dig deep in the pursuit of mastery. It's tough, if not impossible, to be that way all the time in all areas, but it's still a great way to be—especially when it comes to your career.

This kind of curiosity is *vital to becoming unstuck* because, once you find something you are extremely curious about, you will drill down on it until you become an expert. Curiosity is only a starting point. It's about being aware of your curiosities and how those connect to something worth pursuing.

That's the way it's been for me in my career. Contrary to the beliefs of my podcast listeners, I wasn't born an expert in the science of HVAC. I was exposed to a tiny bit of it when I was a kid and became curious about how it worked. I realized that I really liked it, that it was something worth mastering. I was driven forward not by how much I already knew but by the recognition of how much I *didn't* know.

There is this psychological concept called "the illusion of explanatory depth," which is our tendency to believe that we know a lot more about a topic than we actually do. It's only when someone asks us to explain it that we (and everybody else in the room) realize that we really don't understand it at all. Again, this is a tendency that most of us share.

The Yale researchers who coined the term "illusion of explanatory depth" tested their theory through experimentation. They asked a group of study participants to rate their understanding of how zippers work on a scale of one to ten. Most people rated their understanding of zippers pretty high on the scale. The researchers then asked the participants to *explain in detail* how zippers work, and—you guessed it—most of them couldn't do it, at least not to the level of their perceived understanding. It turns out that most people are only mildly curious or knowledgeable about zippers.

> **There is this psychological concept called "the illusion of explanatory depth," which is our tendency to believe that we know a lot more about a topic than we actually do.**

True curiosity, on the other hand, leads you to dig down deep and understand something to the extent that you can explain it—and, hopefully, apply it. That's how you can tell the difference between something you (or your child) are only superficially curious about and something that has the potential to hold your (or their) interest for a lifetime.

For me, that something was HVAC. In fact, my HVAC School website is the result of my curiosity in the pursuit of mastery.

I've made it my job to teach people about the science of HVAC. I know a lot about it, but I also know that there are a lot of things I don't yet know. But I have to be able to explain this stuff to our trainees and students, so as soon as I come across something I can't adequately explain, I hunker down and study it until I can explain it well. And once I get it, I'm super excited to share what I've just learned. *That's* the kind of curiosity I'm talking about.

Curiosity in the pursuit of mastery makes you humble and brave. It gives you confidence. It makes you unafraid to ask questions or be in the presence of people much smarter than you. An unconfident person can't do that because they would feel threatened. But a deeply curious person will always ask those hard questions, have the grit to bust through the difficult moments in pursuit of mastery, and continue to grow for the rest of their life.

Think back to what I said in the "Unstuckable" chapter: It's about shotgunning before lasering—being willing to pursue a lot of things until you stumble upon something that simply will not let you go.

Another way to put it is "wide, narrow, wide." In the initial "wide" phase, you're very curious about everything. You're looking around, seeing all the possibilities, exploring lots of interests. Then you go "narrow" on something long enough to achieve some mastery, get some answers, and make some progress. At that point, you go "wide" again, looking at your results and determining what to do next.

> **Curiosity in the pursuit of mastery makes you humble and brave.**

If there's any danger in this approach, it's the temptation to avoid finishing things. That's why it's good for kids to learn how to complete tasks along the way, to have some kind of time-binding and urgency to their exploration.

For example, I have a nephew who is really into robotics. If he could, he would dive into his curiosity about robotics, not pay mind to anything else, and never come up for air. The cool thing about his involvement in robotics is that it has competitions, which means he must meet deadlines in order to qualify to compete. Milestones provide a realistic binding to his curiosity and force him to move forward in his mastery rather than getting bogged down in the weeds forever—much like that limpkin in the swampy ditch by the side of the road.

13 Feedback vs. Validation

One of my team members walked into my office and asked me if I had time to look at something on my computer that he had been working on. He said he wanted some feedback on it. Now, I knew he had everything he needed to make the right decision and that my opinion mattered little for the success of the project, so I threw him a curve ball.

"You say you want *feedback*," I said to him, "but are you looking for *feedback* or *validation*?"

Jerk move on my part? Maybe, but I wanted him to understand the difference between the two. I also want you to understand it because it's an important concept to keep in mind as you guide children (or yourself) along an educational and career path.

Let's start with **feedback**. I had the chance to do some brief contract work for the blockbuster radio show and podcast *This American Life*. Like most great radio shows, it has a rigorous editorial process in which all the producers sit in a room and give one another feedback (aka opinions, reactions, criticism, and advice) on their stories as

> "You say you want *feedback*," I said to him, "but are you looking for *feedback* or *validation*?"

they are being produced. They call this process an "edit," and most of the producers, as well as the host of the show, Ira Glass, credit the depth of the show's storytelling and production to these intense, well-structured editorial sessions. These meetings are all about giving and receiving real feedback. They can be brutal, but the goal is quality radio, and everyone puts their egos aside for that result.

Contrast that with **validation**. Have you ever emailed or posted something online and then sat staring at the screen, hitting refresh, waiting to see how people will react, and hoping against hope that they will give you a positive response? When we do that (and almost everybody does that!), we are not seeking feedback—we're seeking validation. None of us ever really gets over our desire for affirmation and approval.

Many times, I ask for feedback. Then, when I get it, I feel sad, mad, or want to quit. When that happens, you can be pretty sure I didn't really want feedback but craved validation.

So now, when I'm tempted to ask for feedback, I stop for a second and ask myself, "Do I really want feedback or validation?" If I truly want feedback, great! Now I can create a structure like *This American Life* does with its edit sessions so that I get what I need. And if it's validation I'm after—someone to tell me that everything is okay and I'm doing great—fine! I'll take that request to someone who will give me what I want.

> **Many times, I ask for feedback. Then, when I get it, I feel sad, mad, or want to quit.**

In a nutshell: Feedback requires structure, while validation is best saved for calls to Mom.

Now, why do I think that it's critical for you and your kids to understand the difference between feedback and validation? Well, I've interacted with and trained scores of people in my business, and I've come across many folks whose primary goal is not to learn but to be *seen* as a learner. They only want validation. I can spot them a mile away (and so can every other employer and teacher).

The ones looking for validation don't take the initiative to learn on their own time. They often don't pursue any curiosity. They are not driven by their excitement over the topic at hand. They are driven by being in my face so that I will notice them and make them feel good about themselves.

Here's one tell-tale sign of someone who's only after validation: In our training, when we have a Q&A session with a speaker, the validation-seeker will stand up and, instead of asking a question, will deliver a statement. Maybe they'll make a good point, or maybe they won't. It doesn't matter. If they were really interested in learning from this speaker or from me, they would ask a question.

If you have an opportunity to learn from an expert, you do what it takes to learn from them. As an employer, I want to hire people who want to grow and contribute, not people who are going to be seeking approval all the time.

Some people pursue a degree or multiple degrees because, to them, those pieces of paper are proof that they are capable and authorized. We call these people *perpetual students*, which is not to be confused with *lifelong learners* who seek knowledge that they can apply. Perpetual students are those who learn so that they can accumulate knowledge and feel validated by the vast amount of information they can store in their heads—or by all the people who tell them that they're good or smart. They are constantly seeking affirmation. Sometimes, this is due to something lacking from their youth, while sometimes, it's because they simply crave it internally.

Everybody enjoys a little validation now and then. It's part of the human experience and is a perfectly healthy part of human relationships—but it's worth recognizing in ourselves, whether it's feedback or validation we're after. If it's validation, we're probably going to be disappointed because nobody outside of our closest relationships has that kind of time unless they want something from you.

These topics remind me of the classic *Saturday Night Live* sketch in which fictional self-help guru Stuart Smalley uses daily affirmations to boost his confidence. "I'm good enough, I'm smart enough, and doggone it, people like me," Stuart says to his reflection in the mirror. Although I'm not necessarily a big fan of that sort of self-love stuff, I've got to admit that we sometimes need it. If it helps us believe in ourselves and keeps us from having to call our mothers for affirmation all the time, maybe we can call for better reasons.

What I'm saying is that if you're looking outside yourself for validation and approval, you're going to be disappointed. Teach your kids (and remind yourself) to be in relationships with others not because you need something for yourself but because honest, mutually-beneficial human connection is its own reward.

14 Critical Contrarianism

No discussion of feedback and validation would be complete without a discussion of **critical contrarianism**, which is the idea that we should always be critical of things that can be improved and not be afraid to go against popular opinion. The people who are the most successful in their personal lives and careers—whether they are white-collar or blue-collar workers—have a deep understanding of what this means and also what it doesn't mean.

It's helpful to criticize a problem-solving approach that isn't working, a marketing plan that's not generating sufficient buzz, or a household budget that isn't holding water. *It is **not** good, however, to criticize the people who created or are working on the approach, the marketing plan, or the budget.* The most successful teams, families, or peer groups understand that it's possible to have conflict while simultaneously nurturing personal relationships and fostering growth.

> **Task conflict is a healthy disagreement or debate on ideas, processes, or strategies.**

As a dad and business owner, I teach my kids, my employees, and our apprentices about two kinds of conflict: **task conflict** and **personal conflict**.

Task conflict is a healthy disagreement or debate on ideas, processes, or strategies aimed at finding the most effective way to achieve a goal. We love this kind of conflict because it leads to growth.

On the other hand, personal conflict arises from negative emotions or interpersonal issues, often unrelated to the task at hand. This kind of conflict leads to hurt feelings, grudges, and in some unfortunate cases, a black eye or worse.

It's crucial that we teach our children to recognize the difference between these two types of conflicts. Then, we can model and teach them how to maintain positive environments and relationships where task conflicts can take place without leading to personal conflicts.

An example of how task conflicts can be beneficial at work is when two team members have different ideas about how to tackle a project. By openly discussing and challenging each other's ideas, they can uncover innovative solutions and ultimately create a more successful outcome. This process should never be seen as a personal attack but rather as a collaborative effort to improve and reach their highest potential.

To engage in rigorous communication that leads to growth, kids need to cultivate certain character keys:

- **Open-mindedness**: being willing to listen to different perspectives and ideas
- **Respect**: treating everyone with kindness and respect, regardless of disagreements
- **Clarity**: being clear and concise when expressing thoughts or opinions
- **Humility**: acknowledging limitations and staying open to learning from others

Remember that feedback and pushback are essential for growth. When people challenge one another respectfully and constructively, they create opportunities for improvement and development. That's why my company holds project post-mortem meetings that enable us to learn from our experiences and grow as a team. We hold these meetings after the completion of a project—or when something goes wrong—to analyze what worked, what didn't, and how we can improve moving forward.

You can do something similar in your family to help your kids learn valuable skills that will serve them well not only in their careers but also in their relationships. Be sure to:

- model and encourage open and honest communication
- focus on process and outcomes rather than criticizing individuals
- identify areas of improvement for the future
- celebrate successes and acknowledge efforts

In doing so, you will be teaching your kids how to become valued members of any team and not be That Person.

We all know That Person. He's either the follower and conflict avoider who never asks hard questions and never pushes back even when he *knows* something is wrong, or she's the one who attacks colleagues with hurtful, thoughtless opinions and then finishes them off by saying she's "sorry if you can't handle the truth."

There's no place for either of Those People in business or anywhere else. Instead, you'll always find room for other, nicer people who know how to be humble, thoughtful, and kind yet still be willing to practice critical contrarianism when the situation calls for it.

15 Taste and Crappy Work

I have always been fascinated with audio stories. I loved listening to talk radio and kids' radio drama and recording voice and sound when I was a kid. Later, I discovered podcasts, and my mind was blown. One of my early favorite podcasts was the show I mentioned earlier, *This American Life* with Ira Glass. I dreamed of getting into podcasting and becoming the next Ira Glass, so I put on my autodidact hat (which, at the time, kind of resembled a dunce cap since I was a total novice!) and began studying the form.

I listened to every podcast I could find. The ones I loved the most were highly narrative, heavily edited, and had outstanding audio. I conducted research into the best recorders, microphones, techniques, and all the stuff that goes into professional podcasting. Then I invested in the best equipment I could afford. I knew it was not going to be easy to break into the industry, but I was determined to give it a try.

Then, I went to a conference about podcasting, where I learned of a platform that made it possible to be "discovered" as The Next Great Podcast Wunderkind. All you had to do was sign up for this service, which was kind of like an online job board, where you could apply for freelance gigs as a "tape sync" or "stringer" for radio shows and podcasts. Your job was to act as a local audio technician for the show, which might be based a thousand miles away.

The shows couldn't afford to fly their audio people around the country for every story, so they would contract with local techs to do the recordings. As a stringer, you would take your recorder and microphone, travel to the person who was going to be interviewed over the phone by the podcast folks, and record that person's side of the conversation. Meanwhile, the producers on the other end of the phone line were in the studio, recording their side. When they edited the two recordings together, it would make for nice audio.

Being a stringer sounds simple, but it's not. You have to understand audio, have a great microphone and recorder, and make sure no distractions or noises interfere with the sound quality.

My first gig was for a popular podcast called *99% Invisible* produced by Roman Mars out of Oakland, California. My first mission, as I chose to accept it, was to drive from my home in Central Florida to nearby Tampa and audio-record a gentleman who had been arrested for failing to maintain his lawn according to community standards.

The title of the episode was "Lawn Order," in case any of you want to look it up. When a representative from the show called to discuss the assignment with me, he asked what kind of microphone I would be using. I had several different mics at the time, so I fumbled and bumbled and told him what mic gear I planned to use. His response was that my gear was not appropriate for field recording.

"Clearly, you don't have the right gear," he said with a sigh. "I'm afraid this isn't going to work out."

"But I have other microphones!" I exclaimed. "Please, just give me a chance. I'll make it work!"

Reluctantly, he awarded me the gig and gave me the address in Tampa for the home of the man I was supposed to record. There, I knocked on the door and was greeted by a chorus of barking dogs and the subject of our story, an older gentleman who was dripping in sweat. As he tried in vain to get his dogs to be quiet, he told me that the air conditioning in the house was broken (ironically). There was no way we would be able to record anything in that house.

> **As hard as I tried, I could never make them come out the way I wanted.**

I got the producer on the phone and told him what was happening. He suggested we record the interview in my car. We tested it out, but the engine and air conditioning noises were too loud. I would need to shut off the car if I wanted to capture professional-grade audio.

So this old gentleman and I ended up using a 100-degree car as an audio booth for an hour. By the time we were done, we were completely drenched—but the audio came out great. The producer was happy with it, and so was I.

That was the start of my addiction to high-quality narrative audio, and it led me to a season of stringer/tape-sync work for WNYC, *This American Life,* and *Radiotopia*. I produced a couple of podcasts, including one for the Podcast Movement Conference (the largest annual podcast industry summit).

I had a grand vision for these shows, but as hard as I tried, I could never make them come out the way I wanted. It was maddening. I had put so much time into this. I had read the books. I had listened to podcasts about how to make podcasts. I had researched, studied, and tested, yet I remained fundamentally unhappy with the quality of the work I was producing. I was so frustrated.

And then, I stumbled upon a presentation by Ira Glass of *This American*

Life that changed my perspective. In an interview on *The Positive Creatives*, another podcast, Glass talked about how people of good taste are often the most dissatisfied with their work because it doesn't live up to the quality they are striving to achieve:

> *Nobody tells people who are beginners—and I really wish somebody had told this to me—is that all of us who do creative work, we get into it, and we get into it because we have good taste. But it's like there's a gap—that for the first couple of years you're making stuff, what you're making isn't so good, it's not that great. It's trying to be good, it has the ambition to be good, but it's not quite that good.*
>
> *But your taste—the thing that got you into the game— your taste is still killer! And your taste is good enough that you can tell that what you're making is kind of a disappointment to you.*
>
> *A lot of people never get past that phase. A lot of people, at that point, they quit. And the thing that I would just like to say to you with all my heart is that most everybody I know who does interesting creative work... went through a phase of years where they had really good taste, [so] they could tell what they were making wasn't as good as they wanted it to be. They knew it fell short. It didn't have this special thing that we wanted it to have.*
>
> *And the thing that I would say to you is everybody goes through that. And for you to go through it, if you're going through it right now, if you're just getting out of that phase, is you gotta know it's totally normal. And the most important possible thing you can do is do a lot of work. Do*

> *a huge volume of work. Put yourself on a deadline so that every week or every month, you know you're going to finish one story.*
>
> *Because it's only by going through an actual volume of work that you're actually going to catch up and close that gap. And the work that you're making will be as good as you're ambitions. It takes a while. It's going to take you a while. It's normal to take a while. And you just have to fight your way through that.*

Thanks to the wisdom of Ira Glass, I came to understand that if we create something and we're satisfied with it, that's not necessarily a sign that our work was great. It may be a sign that our taste hasn't been cultivated enough. Dissatisfaction with where we are doesn't necessarily come from discontent. It can also be the byproduct of a taste that is ever-evolving.

When you look back at something you created five years ago and feel embarrassed by it, that's a good sign. It means you've grown and are still growing. Obviously, that can be overdone if it leads to regret, but having some degree of dissatisfaction with your work is not necessarily a bad thing.

I tell you this because many people let that sort of dissatisfaction stop them from breaking through to autodidacticism. I get it. It's easier to follow someone else's directions than to create something new on your own. It's like the first time you create artwork or try to play an instrument. You know you suck at it, and that feels bad. Moving away from creative work into something safe and pre-organized feels so much more comfortable.

But here's the thing we miss sometimes: It's actually worse if you can't tell that you suck because then you can't see the distance between where you are now and where you could be, and that is a necessary part of being able to do good work. To do good work takes having enough taste to know that most of your work is crappy.

> *Manual labor, when approached with intention and care, reveals itself as a medium for the soul to express its inherent creativity.*
>
> ~ Mike Rowe

Life should be about more than just doing whatever is laid out for you by other people. It should be about forming your own path, one way or another, and developing your autodidactic chops. Then and only then can you channel your dissatisfaction with the status quo into creating something fierce, something original, something that is uniquely **you**.

16 Parting Words

Thank you for sticking with me all the way to the end! I hope my slightly unusual message about our education system, alternative career paths, and even limpkins has resonated with you in some way.

The aim of my writing is to encourage you to take an active role in instilling character, growth, joy, and purpose in your children so they will have the tools to succeed in any vocation. I hope:

- that you'll encourage them to "shotgun before they laser" so that they can have all kinds of cool experiences while they're still young and open to any possibility
- that you'll introduce them to the beauty of autodidacticism so that their curiosity can lead them forward toward mastery
- that you'll teach them how reps make gains and encourage them to create (and be inspired by) the cartoons in their head

But most of all, I hope that you'll open the door for the young people in your life to follow an unconventional education or career path if that's what they choose. (Maybe you'll even consider opening that door for yourself if it makes sense for you.)

By abandoning expectations and outdated opinions about what makes for a rewarding career—by disregarding peer pressure and the fruitless competition to see whose kid is the most "successful"—you'll give your children the greatest gift of all.

That gift is **freedom**—freedom to be who they truly are at their core and freedom to pursue a career that not only satisfies their soul and rewards them financially for their skills and talents but also makes a real difference in their community.

To do otherwise—to try to shoehorn them into a prestigious role simply because it boosts your parental sense of self—is wrong. It will damage them and your relationship with them.

And remember, they are going to be choosing your nursing home someday.

Our children are not here to serve at the pleasure of our egos. They are here to live their lives and contribute to society in their own unique way.

> I hope that you'll open the door for the young people in your life to follow an unconventional education or career path if that's what they choose.

So have standards for your children but not expectations. Recognize and celebrate the boundless possibilities they represent!

Again—one last time for the people in the back row—I am in no way saying that college is a bad choice for everyone. I don't want to come off as anti-anything. Rather, I am pro-exploration and pro-analysis. I advocate for young people who do not automatically take the traditional path laid out for them without questioning it first. Ideally, open-minded adults whose egos are in check will be there to guide them. That's what I'm saying.

So take the burden off your shoulders, parents. Have freewheeling conversations with your kids about all the possibilities available to them, and help them decide what's best for each of them. If, after careful analysis, they choose to pursue a college education, by all means, do whatever you can to make that work for them. But if that's not the direction they end up choosing, be okay with their choice because it is absolutely okay.

If you can embrace their choice, you're going to have a lot less conflict, a much better relationship with your son or daughter, and your young adult is going to do really well. How bad could that be?

And lastly, I sincerely hope that this book has inspired you to think differently about tradespeople and artisans so that the next time you encounter one, you'll feel compelled to thank them—maybe even tell them how much you value their expertise and recognize the critical role they play in keeping our society running. You could even take it a step further and stand up for them when you hear others disparaging them. By elevating the trades and tradespeople, you'll be doing something great—not just for them but also for our society—because in the wise words of Nelson Mandela:

> *A society thrives when it values the contributions of its skilled laborers and nurtures the crafts that have shaped its history.*

Appendix

RECOMMENDED READING

For me, some of the most inspiring books are the biographies of people who paved their own paths to success. Here are a few you might consider reading:

Sam Walton: Made in America by Sam Walton and John Huey
In this insightful memoir, Walmart founder Sam Walton recounts his journey from a small-town businessman to the head of a global retail empire. The book offers a first-hand look at Walton's unique leadership style, innovative strategies, and unyielding commitment to his values.

Crucial Conversations: Tools for Talking When Stakes Are High by Kerry Patterson, Joseph Grenny, Ron McMillan, and Al Switzler
This book equips readers with practical tools to effectively handle high-stakes conversations where opinions vary and emotions run high. It provides techniques to foster open dialogue, helping you achieve desired outcomes without damaging relationships.

Paddle Your Own Canoe: One Man's Fundamentals for Delicious Living by Nick Offerman
Offerman shares his humorous and poignant journey from a small-town boy to a Hollywood celebrity, highlighting his love for woodworking and the outdoors. His tales underscore the importance of self-reliance, integrity, and living a fulfilling life.

Antifragile: Things That Gain from Disorder by Nassim Nicholas Taleb
Taleb introduces "antifragility," a concept about how certain systems thrive in chaos and disorder. Through various examples, he demonstrates

how embracing randomness and volatility can lead to growth and resilience.

Shop Class as Soulcraft: An Inquiry Into the Value of Work by Matthew B. Crawford

This thought-provoking book champions the value of trade skills and manual labor. Crawford shares his personal experience as a motorcycle mechanic, arguing that such work can be intellectually stimulating, financially rewarding, and socially valuable.

The Challenger Sale: Taking Control of the Customer Conversation by Matthew Dixon and Brent Adamson

Dixon and Adamson present a revolutionary approach to sales, challenging traditional relationship-building methods. The book reveals how successful salespeople challenge customers' thinking, tailoring solutions and taking control of the sales conversation.

Hangry: A Startup Journey by Mike Evans

In this behind-the-scenes account, GrubHub co-founder Mike Evans narrates his startup journey, detailing the challenges, successes, and lessons learned. The story gives a real-world perspective on the grit and resilience required to change an industry.

RECOMMENDED PODCASTS

How I Built This

In this entertaining NPR podcast, the host interviews entrepreneurs about how they built their businesses. It's full of fun, inspiring stories from people who have marched to the beat of their own drums to make amazing lives for themselves.

Hidden Brain

This podcast uses science and storytelling to reveal the unconscious patterns that drive human behavior, shape our choices, and direct our relationships.

The Way I Heard It
This podcast with host Mike Rowe started by telling amazing short stories from history but has morphed into an interview podcast with many unheralded people doing incredible things.

Acknowledgments

Thanks to:

My uncle Keith Huntington for being my first real employer and one of the people I have always looked up to

My mom for being the hardest-working person I've ever met and loving us all unconditionally

My grandmother (Honey) Betty Huntington, for being a model of fun, dignity, and wisdom

My friend, Josh Berg, and his dad, Kevin, for demonstrating what a hard day's work is and living lives of steady commitment to God, family, and work

My trade school instructor Ron Cary for never just giving me the answer

My brother Nathan for always making me laugh and putting up with me

My father-in-law Stan for choosing his family over money time and time again

My mother-in-law Gail for being an example of joy in all things and being so willing to laugh even at herself

Jesse Claerbout for working tirelessly to solve issues he didn't create

Mike Klokus for being a great friend through thick and thin, even when I'm a dime-a-dozen boss

Leslie Broadbent for teaching what work and efficiency mean to so many at Kalos

Bert Testerman for being a great friend and an excellent listener

Kelly Klotz and Ernie Stadden for giving a 17-year-old kid a chance in the HVAC business

Dave Barefoot for giving me a body of jokes to draw from and being my mentor in the trade

Nevin Wertenberger for teaching me how to use a spreadsheet and giving me the space and guidance to grow

Richard Fortin for showing a punk kid the kindness of opportunity and modeling dedication as a leader

Keith Ledford for being encouraging during a tough time in business

Rick Corbin and Nancy Clutts for creating a space for me to come into conflict with myself and become better

Jared Easley for giving me the opportunity to connect with a broader world and teaching me about the power of noticing

Jim Bergmann for being a friend who was always willing to tell me where I needed to learn

Bill Spohn for trusting that I wasn't insane even when I was

Neil Comparetto for being an authentic friend and choosing the best over the easy

Andrew Greaves because you are one of the few people I feel I can be myself with

Acknowledgments

Jordan Cummings because you let me win a race and for being a great guy in general

Regan Murphy for being a steadfast defender and kind friend

The HVAC School admins, moderators, and contributors, all my countless HVAC friends, all the Kalos team, all of the Kalos valued clients, and everyone I've known and met through podcasting and social media. There are far too many to name, but I am grateful for all the support and kindness from all of you.

But most of all...

My kids, for rolling their eyes and knowing how imperfect I am but still letting me do things like this without throwing too much shade

Alex for his patience, Gavin for his curiosity, Elise for her warmth, Maya for her fire, Violet for her kindness, Annora for her creativity, Jude for his thoughtfulness, Margot for her spunk, Sail for his joy, and Bryn for her hard-won affection

Leilani for being a beautiful light and the voice in my head since I was 12. I have no idea who or what I would be without you. IYKYK.

About the Author

Bryan Orr, a self-effacing small business owner, father of ten, and husband of one, has spent a lifetime embracing the challenges of entrepreneurship, family, and the skilled trades. Co-founding Kalos Services—an HVAC, electrical, and construction business in central Florida—with his father and uncle in 2005, Bryan has led the company from a scrappy team of three to a thriving family business with over 250 employees. Along the way, he's navigated the emotional minefield of working with over two dozen family members, accumulating plenty of war stories and wisdom to share along the way.

As a speaker, writer, and mentor, Bryan regularly discusses his experiences and insights about making a family business thrive in the modern world. He's also a self-proclaimed audio nerd with a penchant for podcasting and audio production. In 2016, he launched the website HVAC School (https://hvacrschool.com), a free online training resource for HVAC and refrigeration professionals, which has flourished thanks to the generosity and expertise of its guest contributors.

With bylines in various online publications such as The Good Men Project, Entrepreneur.com, Smallbusiness.com, and Smallbizbonfire.com, Bryan continues to explore the intersection of business, family, and the skilled trades. And though he's learned a great deal through his own experiences, he's the first to admit that he's still figuring things out and learning something new daily.

When he's not wearing one of his many professional hats, Bryan can be found at home in rural central Florida, enjoying the chaos and love of his large family. He lives with his wife Leilani and eight of their ten children (Elise, Maya, Violet, Annora, Jude, Margot, Sail, and Bryn), relishing the adventure of raising the next generation of skilled laborers, entrepreneurs and, most importantly, compassionate human beings.

www.ingramcontent.com/pod-product-compliance
Lightning Source LLC
Chambersburg PA
CBHW031404160426
43196CB00007B/888